STRENGTH IN ADVERSITY

A BIBLICAL STUDY

Donna E. Lane, Ph.D.

W. David Lane, Ph.D.

ISBN 978-1986823043

Bear's Place Publishing
Snellville, Georgia, USA

CONTENTS

Acknowledgements

We wish to acknowledge the invaluable contributions of Andie Newell, Deborah and Jim Chambers, and Connie Mitchell, who offered feedback and editing prior to publication.

We want to acknowledge all the wounding, betrayals, abuses, rejections, and losses, which taught us these priceless lessons on how to stand in the face of adversity. In full knowledge that everything that happens is redeemed by God, we wish to thank you.

We also want to thank each other, for patiently working side by side to create this study, and for sharing in the journey of this life with love, support, and faithfulness.

Finally, we wish to thank our son, Cody. He was the brightest example of dealing with adversity with strength, character, perseverance, peace, and joy we have ever witnessed. We miss him.

Dedication

TO CODY

Your life was, and continues to be, a light shining in the darkness, pointing everyone in your sphere of influence toward the One True Source. Your relationship with Jesus was the deepest, most intimate example of oneness with Christ we have known.

We are looking forward to the end of the interim.

STRENGTH IN ADVERSITY

BEFORE WE BEGIN

Life is difficult, and filled with adversity. Adversity takes many forms. Because we are each a unique, one-of-a-kind creation of God, we experience suffering differently, based on how we are made, our history, and our developmental stage. For example, a sensitive soul who has never been seriously wounded, and who goes through rejection in middle school, will respond very differently from a warrior spirit who has suffered childhood abuse or neglect who experiences rejection during middle age. Even the same type of adversity, such as the death of a loved one, is experienced uniquely by each individual.

In this study, we have chosen to identify adversity as represented by different places or events, using Scriptural locations and stories to distinguish different types of adversity. Egypt, for example, was the land where the Israelites lived in slavery (Exodus 3:7); thus, Egypt indicates some type of bondage, ranging from the slavery of addiction to serving money as god in our lives. The Wilderness, where the Israelites wandered for 40 years due to their lack of trust in God (Numbers 32:13), indicates suffering from desires remaining just out of reach, and feelings of separation or distance from God. Babylon represents walking through fire (Daniel 3:16-23) – any intense, overwhelming single event that threatens to consume us.

The Valley (Psalm 23) is the anguish of walking through illness, or toward death, including your own, or the fear of any impending loss. The Cave, the hiding place of David (I Samuel

22:1), represents the isolation caused by self-protection, losing ourselves through hiding, or covering our true nature with a mask. Berakah, the location where Jehoshaphat faced three different armies all attacking at once (II Chronicles 20:22-26), represents those times when Satan, the enemy, comes against us on all sides and piles on one calamity after another, just like the Southern old wives' tale of bad things coming in threes. The Storm, where the disciples, out on the sea, panicked in fear and their doubt took over (Luke 8:22-25), represents those times when chaos swirls and rages around us and we feel we are foundering.

Then, we come to the sufferings of Christ. The Desert, where Jesus was tempted by Satan (Matthew 4:1-10), represents lack, such as a lack of basic needs being met, a lack of love, affection, or valuing, or a temptation to meet our needs with something other than God. The Gates, where Jesus cried to take Israel under His wings (Luke 13:34-35), represents observing the pain and suffering of someone else, particularly someone we love, and feeling powerless to stop it. The Tomb of Lazarus (John 11:38-39, 43-44) represents the experience of grief and loss. Gethsemane (Matthew 26:36-39) is the anticipation of impending pain and suffering, and our struggling to face it. And Calvary (Luke 23:33) represents suffering on behalf of someone else, because of sacrifice for them, because of their sin against you, because of rejection, or because of false accusation against you or belief about you.

Perhaps you have noticed by now that each of these Scriptural stories of adversity follows the same theme: adversity is followed by redemption. The Israelites were released from slavery in Egypt, walking through the waters to freedom. After wandering in the Wilderness, the children of Israel entered the Promised Land. Shadrach, Meshach, and Abednego were met in the fiery furnace and walked out untouched by the flames.

STRENGTH IN ADVERSITY

The Valley of the shadow of death of Psalm 23 is described as a place without fear, because God is there, comforting us and caring for us. David emerged from his hiding place, the Cave, to take his true identity as a man after God's own heart, King of Israel, and father to Messiah's lineage. Jehoshaphat sent his singers before the armies of Israel into the valley of Berakah to praise God, and there, the three enemies turned on each other and were destroyed without Israel even having to fire one arrow. In the midst of the Storm on the sea, Jesus remained at complete peace, rose up, and calmed the sea with a word.

In the Desert, Jesus responded with truth to each enemy lie, and resisted all temptations. Although Israel did not receive Jesus as their Messiah when Jesus cried out for it, He did make it possible for His children – even the Gentiles – to rest under His wings by ransoming them from the clutches of sin. Jesus wept in genuine anguish at Lazarus' death, and at the inevitability of death because of the fallen nature of this world, but promptly raised Lazarus, demonstrating that death has no power anymore. Jesus prayed at Gethsemane, and came to a place of peace, acceptance, and resolution. And the cross resulted in the resurrection, the final defeat of sin and death, and the ultimate victory over evil.

This book follows the same theme: adversity is met by Jesus Christ with redemption. Why, then, do we have such difficulty standing in the face of adversity? Why do we try to avoid difficulty at all costs? Why do we fear pain? What blocks our vision of the redemptions of God? What are the causes of suffering in our lives, and what are the consequences of suffering? How do we walk through suffering rejoicing, as Paul describes (Romans 5:3, Colossians 1:24)?

We will address these questions, and explore in depth what Scripture reveals about the nature, causes, and consequences of suffering, and how to navigate adversity without losing ourselves or being overcome by it, while remaining in the peace of Christ. Using the different scriptural stories of adversity we have outlined as points of reference, we will process how to remain in the joy of the presence of Christ, no matter the circumstances. We will describe how to fight the enemy effectively, and how to stand in the strength of God, made perfect in our weakness (II Corinthians 12:9), when difficulty comes.

The book is divided into sections, and each section contains the following components: Scripture verses relevant to the section topic; a writing examining concepts presented in the Scriptures in depth, on a theme or question related to adversity; prayer questions to bring to the Lord; meditations for further contemplation; and, processing through synthesis (combining the concepts to create a whole), and application (practical use of the concepts in daily life). Each section is designed to take a week to complete, but be flexible with yourself or your group, and with the process, taking as much time as needed to fully receive everything the Lord has for you in your journey.

Begin by reading the Scripture verses for the section. Many of the verses may be familiar to you, but take time to read them anew, not just by rote, and consider their application to facing adversity. Take the time to look up each verse, and read several verses leading up to and following the selection to see the context. Ask what the Lord is wanting to say to you in those verses. Look deeper than the obvious or surface meaning, because the Holy Spirit can breathe new revelation and understanding each time we open our hearts to His truth.

Next, read the writing for the section. You may want to read through it once, and go back over it a second time more deliberately, focusing on any points that bring up questions for you or lead to new insights. We suggest having a notebook to use with this study to write down any questions you have as they arise. You can also use it to take notes on the key points you want to remember.

Once you have fully absorbed the ideas presented in the writing, set aside time to spend in prayer with the Lord, using the questions provided along with any questions that came up for you during the reading. Allow substantial time for listening for His responses to your questions. This process may take several days, focusing on one question at a time, or you may choose to have a lengthier "get away" for deep meditation and prayer where you wait in solitude to hear from the Lord. If you do not readily hear from the Lord, do not press in to the point of feeling frustrated with the process. Instead, ask the Lord to show you what may be in the way of you hearing Him, feeling His presence, or receiving His truth in your heart. The enemy consistently interferes in our attempts to hear from Jesus, so do not allow Satan to blame or condemn you if you do not hear readily. Keep in mind, the more we seek Him, the better our "reception" tunes in to His voice. Jesus does speak to you, and will speak to you in the way that is both most beneficial for you and most readily received by you. The Lord may bring answers to your questions at any point throughout the day or week, in a variety of ways. So, remain open to whatever and however He responds. When the Lord speaks to your heart in response to your seeking Him, follow wherever He leads you; do not feel you must rigidly follow the questions provided in the book, as they are suggestions only and may not be relevant to what the Lord wants to reveal to you.

As you receive additional truth and insight from the Lord, begin to contemplate the meditations. You may find these meditations align with the Lord's leading, and truth you are receiving from Him. These meditations are designed to help you integrate His truth deeply into your heart until it becomes part of your regular thoughts, feelings, and perspectives.

Processing concepts at the end of each section builds one upon another to develop an overarching approach to responding to adversity. This segment is divided into synthesis and application. The goal is for you to grasp concepts, not develop a list of steps to take or rules to follow. If you understand the concepts, you will be able to see the whole picture, and can better understand any of its parts and apply the information presented to your own life. First, process the information you have gleaned from each section by synthesizing the main beliefs and attitudes you want to adopt. You may use the ones provided, and add your own based on your takeaways. Take each concept and include it as a point of focus for your spiritual journey. Then, process the information by applying the concepts through actions. These applications give suggested ways to respond to adversity, based on the attitudes and beliefs you adopt. Be intentional and specific in how you apply the concepts to your daily life, particularly when adversity comes; however, remember, these applications are not a list of steps to follow. Instead, think of the process as a cache of weapons you can use in battle, and choose your actions based on what works for you.

As you move through each section of the book, continue to practice earlier concepts as you add new beliefs, attitudes, and applications to your arsenal. At the end of the study, you will have a cohesive way to respond to adversity that strengthens you to stand on truth and remain in His peace, no matter what your circumstances.

This book can be used as a study for small groups or Sunday school classes, as a book study, or as a personal journey of exploration and growth. In whatever way it is utilized, we pray, at the end of the journey, you will find yourself more intimately connected with Jesus, more certain of His love for you, filled with His joy, and enfolded in the warm embrace of His peace.

STRENGTH IN ADVERSITY

ONE

THE NARROW ROAD

Scripture

Remember to take time to read each verse carefully and in depth, not by rote, and to consider their application to facing adversity. Look up each verse, and read several verses leading up to and following the selection to understand the context. Ask what the Lord is wanting to say to you as you read these verses.

I Corinthians 16:13-14 Be on your guard; stand firm in the faith; be courageous; be strong. Do everything in love.

II Corinthians 1:21-22 Now it is God who makes both us and you stand firm in Christ. He anointed us, set his seal of ownership on us, and put his Spirit in our hearts as a deposit, guaranteeing what is to come.

Galatians 5:1 It is for freedom that Christ has set us free. Stand firm, then, and do not let yourselves be burdened again by a yoke of slavery.

Matthew 7:13-14 *"Enter through the narrow gate. For wide is the gate and broad is the road that leads to destruction, and many enter through it. But small is the gate and narrow the road that leads to life, and only a few find it."*

Luke 14:27-28, 33 *"And whoever does not carry their cross and follow me cannot be my disciple. Suppose one of you wants to build a tower. Won't you first sit down and estimate the cost to see if you have enough money to complete it? In the same way, those of you who do not give up everything you have cannot be my disciples."*

Enter Through the Narrow Gate

Why do so many of us struggle to stand in the face of adversity? The truth is, we have a problem with pain. We take issue with it. We fear it. We avoid it whenever we can, basically at all costs. We rail against it. We get annoyed, frustrated, and grumpy when we are in it. We try our best to ignore it, and remain in denial. We get confused and overwhelmed when we suffer because of it. We desire a pain-free existence.

We often teach our children that pain is very bad, sometimes overtly by overreacting when they are hurt, and sometimes inadvertently by trying to protect them from ever experiencing difficulty, if we can help it. We, ourselves, believe that the easy road is best, and we pass this belief on to our children by excusing them from hardship and rescuing them from the consequences of their choices. Thus, the belief that pain is a problem is passed on from one generation to the next.

STRENGTH IN ADVERSITY

Our society reinforces the idea that pain in unacceptable and to be avoided. Advertisements for medications for pain inundate us with this message overtly and subliminally. As one comedian quipped, "Something wrong with your head? Two in the mouth – pop pop." It is not only socially acceptable, but socially expected that everyone will drink alcohol in social situations; again, the unstated message is we all need something to make us comfortable and at ease, because facing interaction without assistance is too difficult.

In our own lives, we seek ease and comfort, and we elevate safety as one of our highest values, perhaps even a higher value than truth. When faced with potential adversity, we like choosing the wide gate, the broad road. Jesus refers to this road as the one that leads to destruction. However, our desire seems to have become to avoid pain at any cost, believing anything that is difficult must be bad, even if that broad road ultimately leads to our annihilation. God looks at it differently. He doesn't choose based on easy or safe; He chooses based on what is best for us. God always chooses based on love, even when loving us is hard or painful for Him. The cross is the best evidence of this truth.

Because of our desire for the easy road, we can develop an uncanny ability to blame others, to avoid taking responsibility, and to never learn the consequences of our choices or how to ask forgiveness and make amends for our actions toward others. How can we, under these parameters, embrace relationship? The truth is, if we believe the easy road is for us, we are not going to invest in relationships at all. Relationships are hard, require effort, and can be painful things. What we learn from the easy path is selfish behavior, which precludes relationship. This is not love. And this is not God. God seeks relationship with us, and will do whatever it takes for the sake of who He loves.

Unlike God, we tend to make our choices based on self-centered motives. We don't want to give up our self-protection or our self-justification. We hold tightly to our defenses like they are life preservers instead of millstones around our neck. We expect Jesus to take care of problems for us, like a fairy godmother, or prevent bad things from happening, like a magician; yet, we do not want to walk the Kingdom road, which He has shown includes carrying a cross. The Kingdom road looks difficult to us. The Kingdom road is painful. The Kingdom road has a cost.

It is difficult to love as Jesus calls us to love. It is a struggle to love our enemies. It is hard to forgive those who have harmed us and pray for those who persecute us (Matthew 5:44). Our hearts ache in fear when we begin to put ourselves out there, to be vulnerable, open, and genuine with others. We don't want to risk it, because we have felt the pain of rejection and mistreatment at the hands of others, and we don't want to face that feeling again. It is also painful to face our faults and flaws, to humble ourselves and admit wrongdoing, to take responsibility for our choices and to make things right when we have done wrong. Doing these things feels like a threat to our identity.

So, we do our best to avoid challenging circumstances, deep relationships, and anything else that risks suffering and adversity. Fear becomes the voice that directs our path, and we get lost in the fog the fear produces. We are left with the false perception we are alone, stumbling blindly along the broad road. Under the relentless and many-faceted antagonisms of the voice of fear, we begin to react instead of choosing, at times forgetting we even have a choice. As a result, when we are faced with climbing a steep mountain to get out of the Valley, we settle for remaining in the shadows. When we are beset by a raging Storm, we cover our heads and hide in the bowels of our boat, and we cry out in anger at God, wondering where He is and why He isn't doing something, just like the disciples did. When someone hurts us, we hide ourselves in a Cave in our hearts, hoping we are not seen or found out, and in so doing, we forget who we are. Rather than letting go of the ways we use to try to fill the emptiness within us, we seek to return to slavery in Egypt and grip tightly to our many addictions and idols.

We want to turn away from the prospect of warfare, rather than walking into Berakah praising God, ready to fight as He instructs, unaware that we are choosing the darkness over the light. We ache for our heart's desires, but when the time comes, rather than facing whatever giants are in that land, we put aside our true desires to avoid being disappointed, and continue to wander aimlessly in the Wilderness like the Israelites. We kneel at the altar to false gods rather than risk the fiery furnace of the judgments of others, justifying it to ourselves as necessary so we do not appear judgmental, weird, or crazy.

We pursue our self-gratification over carrying the cross of our Calvary by putting someone else first. In the Desert of enemy temptations, Satan entices us to follow our feelings and excuse our failings, claiming we cannot help it and convincing us we don't have a choice. We want to run from the Gates of sharing in the suffering of others, turning our focus on "fixing" it or making ourselves feel better instead of genuinely being present with those who are in pain. Similarly, in the face of grief, we seek to suppress or even medicate our pain rather than express it and share it with others. We don't pray in our Gethsemane for God's will to be done; the voice of fear is telling us to seek our will and beg God for that outcome.

Jesus promises us in this world we will have trouble (John 16:33). Clearly, the belief that we can have a pain-free, easy path, with no difficulty, struggle, and suffering, is false. Satan uses that lie against us, deceiving us to pray for God to remove our adversity instead of praying for God to walk through adversity with us. "When you ask, you do not receive, because you ask with wrong motives" (James 4:3). Having prayed based on a lie, we soon begin to doubt the efficacy of prayer, which is a short step away from doubting God, His goodness, and His love.

Satan whispers fear in our hearts, and we listen: avoid, hide, run away, he encourages; and we agree. None of these approaches work for us, but we continue to do them anyway. The one thing we do not do in the face of adversity is appreciate it. We cannot imagine pain as a good thing; however, pain is our warning system provided by God. It simply identifies for us when there is something wrong that needs to be addressed. It wakes us up to things that are not good or right or true. It reminds us that this is not our home. It helps us to identify with Christ and to "share in his sufferings in order that we may also share in his glory" (Romans 8:17). If not for pain, we would keep repeating the same problem behaviors, getting injured from the same actions, and failing to correct or take care of issues that are a danger to us. We would not see the enemy's attacks for what they are, since we would feel safe within his traps.

Instead of running from pain, what if we used it? We could even turn Satan's tactics against him, if we would look to the pain to learn what it is telling us and revealing to us about Satan's plans. We could address the causes of our pain, whether they are physical or emotional, circumstantial or relational, and bring the truth of Christ to bear as our weapon against whatever problem is causing our pain. We could turn to Jesus as our comfort in the midst of our pain. "For just as we share abundantly in the sufferings of Christ, so also our comfort abounds through Christ" (II Corinthians 1:5).

The enemy tricks us into seeking safety instead of seeking first the Kingdom of God. Teaching about worry and fear, Jesus said, "seek first His kingdom and His righteousness, and all these things (the safety, security, and comfort of our needs being met) will be given to you as well" (Matthew 6:33). C. S. Lewis explained this important idea in this way: "Look for yourself, and you will find in the long run only hatred, loneliness, despair, rage, ruin, and decay. But look for Christ and you will find Him, and with Him everything else thrown in."[1] As a continuation to Jesus' admonition that we will have trouble in this world, He said, "But take heart! I have overcome the world" (John 16:33).

Jesus has provided the Kingdom of God within us, in the here-and-now (Luke 17:21). However, when we focus on safety, security, or ease and comfort, we are looking to an external place, an outside source, to provide our peace. We cannot create peace within our hearts by seeking safety, ease, or comfort in the world as the motivation for our choices. We will never find joy by avoiding pain and fleeing from adversity. If we live focused on the world, we live outside the Kingdom, because His Kingdom is within.

Jesus described several times how those living outside of the Kingdom would experience "weeping and gnashing of teeth" (Matthew 8:12, 13:42, 13:50, 22:13, 24:51, 25:30; Luke 13:28). He invites us to experience the Kingdom with Him by standing with Him in love against fear, for "perfect love drives out fear" (I John 4:18). He wants to drive out of us anything that causes us to sin, and weed out of us all lies from the enemy, so we may live fully immersed in the Kingdom of God, right here and now in our lives. Living in the Kingdom of God is the one and only way to genuine, lasting peace, and true joy. Are you ready?

Questions for Prayer

We begin now to walk the narrow road by asking the Lord the difficult questions – questions that examine our hearts, our motives, and our beliefs, and reveal where we have faltered in standing firm. Remember, if you do not readily hear from the Lord, be patient with yourself and the process. Do not push to the point of frustration; extend yourself grace, take a break from listening when needed, move on from questions where you are getting stuck, and come back to those questions later.

Be sure to use your notebook to write down responses you receive from the Lord as you pray over each question. Don't trust your memory alone to retain every detail of what He shows you.

Lord, I ask that You would be with me as I seek to listen to Your voice and learn more about standing in the face of adversity. Open my heart to receive Your truth, and guard my heart against the enemy's lies. Show me, Jesus...

1. What are some examples of times in my life when I have listened to fear and sought to avoid pain?

2. In what ways or situations have I chosen an easy path rather than entering through the narrow gate?

3. How have I used other means to deal with pain instead of turning to You?

4. Based on choices You see me making and what You know is in my heart, what do I value most?

5. In what ways am I choosing from a self-centered or self-protective motive?

6. When am I most tempted to respond with defensiveness and justification?

7. How have I hidden my true nature, the person that You created me to be?

8. When have I prayed to You and asked You for intervention with false motives?

9. In what areas in my life have I believed I am entitled to an easy road?

10. What does it mean when You say the Kingdom of God is within me?

Meditations

Spend time contemplating the ideas presented below, always keeping your heart and mind open to the leading of the Lord. Refer to the Scriptures at the beginning of this section as you meditate on these truths. If you have questions about any of these concepts, turn to the Lord in prayer and ask Him for His understanding.

When I walk through Valley and Storm, I have nothing to fear. Fear has to do with judgment, but I am not condemned. No! I am loved, as Your precious child. I am loved perfectly, and perfect love casts out fear.

I am never alone. No matter where my journey takes me, You are with me. You live within my heart, and Your Kingdom resides where You are.

Your Kingdom is here-and-now and is within me. I do not have to wait on heaven to experience Your Kingdom. Your Kingdom has come. Focusing on You within my heart helps me remain in Your Kingdom.

I have been sealed with the presence of the Holy Spirit, Who lives in my heart, and I belong to You. My position in the Kingdom is secured.

When I consider the cost of walking Your narrow path, I recognize that being joined with You is worth any cost, and I am willing to face any adversity, knowing You strengthen me.

Process

Process these suggested areas of focus based on this section. Remember, the goal is for you to grasp concepts, not develop a list of steps to take or rules to follow. If you understand the concepts, you will be able to see the whole picture, and can better understand any of its parts and apply the information presented to your own life. These suggestions may not match concepts that you valued from this section, so add your own concepts, based on beliefs and attitudes you have chosen to adopt from the reading and your time with the Lord, and applications that work for you. Incorporate these concepts in your daily meditations and prayer. Practice recalling each concept during times of adversity, and applying the concepts, with the Lord's help.

Synthesis: I choose to use the enemy's tactics against him, and use pain as my signal to recognize that something is amiss. Instead of avoiding it or running from it, I choose to seek You in it, and listen for Your truth.

Application: When I feel pain:

I will remind myself that the pain is helping me identify something that needs to be addressed;

I will share honestly what I am feeling with the Lord;

I will ask the Lord what the pain is trying to show me;

I will look for the Lord to be with me in my pain.

Synthesis: Rather than looking for safety and security in this world, I choose to focus on You, and allow Your presence to bring my heart to a place of peace and joy.

Application: When I feel fear:

I will pause and take a few deep breaths;

I will recenter myself on truths I already know from the Lord (such as, there is no fear in love);

I will face the fear;

I will ask the Lord what is behind my fear;

I will ask the Lord what His response is to what I am fearing;

I will listen for new truths from the Lord that I need to address the specific fear.

Conclusion

In Section One, we presented a new perspective on adversity, and offered the first of many weapons to use to address pain and fear. We encourage you to slow down and consider the truths presented in this section, allowing those truths to inform your responses, rather than simply reacting to adversity. Responding instead of reacting will help you to remain on the narrow road. As you walk through the Valley, look for Jesus, for He is right there with you. As you brave the Storm, take your eyes off the waves, and focus on Jesus, Who will bring peace to your heart.

Now, let's consider the reasons for and consequences of adversity in our lives, to be better equipped to stand.

TWO

PERSEVERANCE, CHARACTER, & HOPE

Scripture

Remember to take time to read each verse carefully and in depth, not by rote, and to consider their application to facing adversity. Look up each verse, and read several verses leading up to and following the selection to understand the context. Ask what the Lord is wanting to say to you as you read these verses.

Romans 5:3-5 *Not only so, but we also glory in our sufferings, because we know that suffering produces perseverance; perseverance, character; and character, hope. And hope does not put us to shame, because God's love has been poured out into our hearts through the Holy Spirit, who has been given to us.*

Hebrews 12:1-3 *Therefore, since we are surrounded by such a great cloud of witnesses, let us throw off everything that hinders and the sin that so easily entangles. And let us run with perseverance the race marked out for us, fixing our eyes on Jesus, the pioneer and perfecter of faith. For the joy set before him he endured the cross, scorning its shame, and sat down at the right hand of the* *throne of God. Consider him who endured such opposition from sinners, so that you will not grow weary and lose heart.*

Romans 8:18, 28 *I consider that our present sufferings are not worth comparing with the glory that will be revealed in us. And we know that in all things God works for the good of those who love him, who have been called according to his purpose.*

Romans 5:12, 21 *Therefore, just as sin entered the world through one man, and death through sin, and in this way death came to all people, because all sinned — just as sin reigned in death, so also grace might reign through righteousness to bring eternal life through Jesus Christ our Lord.*

II Corinthians 4:7-10, 16-17 *But we have this treasure in jars of clay to show that this all-surpassing power is from God and not from us. We are hard pressed on every side, but not crushed; perplexed, but not in despair; persecuted, but not abandoned; struck down, but not destroyed. We always carry around in our body the death of Jesus, so that the life of Jesus may also be revealed in our body. Therefore, we do not lose heart. Though outwardly we are wasting away, yet inwardly we are being renewed day by day. For our light and momentary troubles are achieving for us an eternal glory that far outweighs them all.*

Romans 6:23 *For the wages of sin is death, but the gift of God is eternal life in Christ Jesus our Lord.*

The Consequences of Sin

Adversity in this life is a direct consequence of the presence of sin: the sin that taints the world from the original sin of Adam and Eve; our own sin and the sins of others against us or that affect us; and, the presence of the enemy inhabiting sin and using deception to influence our choices. Because our spirits live in sin-touched bodies, destined to perish, and our bodies currently exist in a sin-consumed world, adversity is inevitable.

Because adversity is inevitable, we need to realize that, whatever we choose, we will face some sort of adversity. Either we will have the pain that comes from the discipline and sacrifice of following the narrow road of Christ, or we will have the pain of disappointment and emptiness of not having what we want out of life. Since either result is pain, it just makes sense to choose the path that ultimately leads to what we want: peace and joy and love.

Suffering is our physiological and emotional experience resulting from adversity, based on our beliefs about the adversity and our perceptions of it. Whether we suffer because of adversity depends in large part on the beliefs we have about the adversity, about ourselves, and about God. Think about this for a moment: our suffering does not come directly from the adversity we experience, but from our beliefs about the adversity. In other words, how we interpret adversity determines how we feel about it.

Here is a concrete example of what we mean. Our daughter, Lindsey, is a long-distance runner. For Lindsey, the experience of running is joyful and invigorating, producing a deep sense of freedom and accomplishment. She looks forward to that moment all runners reach where it seems her body is about to quit on her, when she pushes herself past her apparent limits, only to experience new energy, even exhilaration, just around the next bend. Surely, her body hurts during her long runs, but the joy outweighs any physical pain, so much so she barely notices it.

However, her Momma and Daddy have a very different belief about running. To us, running feels almost abusive to our bodies, and our minds despise the thought of it. We perceive running as unnecessary pain, and a waste of time. If we ever try to run, we hit the proverbial wall almost immediately, and quickly choose to walk the remainder of the course. We experience none of the joy or freedom our daughter describes; instead, we feel intense pain at the outset, and do not persevere or overcome. For us, the pain is the only thing we notice from the experience.

What Lindsey believes about running determines her experience of the suffering produced in her body and mind by running. Similarly, our negative experience of running comes directly from our perceptions of running, and our level of pain matches our beliefs. Clearly, in this example, the same adversity (long-distance running) produces very different experiences, based solely on the beliefs and perceptions of the individuals participating. This concept is critical to our understanding of the Scriptures on suffering.

Paul's writings on suffering in Romans, II Corinthians, and other letters indicate our experiences of adversity can vary profoundly. He experienced bondage in prison (Egypt), walking through several kinds of fire (Babylon), doubt (Storm), impending death (Valley), and isolation (Cave). He knew what it was like to have desires just out of reach (Wilderness) and to have great lack (Desert). He wrote extensively about his heart aching for the people he taught (Gates) and his own suffering on their behalf (Calvary). Yet, he said suffering does not have to be a bad experience. In fact, he professes his own joy in the face of suffering, the good fruit produced by suffering, and the glory revealed through suffering for the Kingdom.

Many of us balk at the ideas of suffering producing good fruit, like perseverance, character, and hope, and glorying in our suffering. Those ideas sound like foolishness to us. Some of us even get angry at hearing these ideas, as if God is diminishing or minimizing our experience of suffering. Frankly, we simply don't want to suffer, but because we don't understand the cause of adversity, the consequences of sin, and the impact of our own beliefs on our experience of suffering, we are easily deceived by the enemy into anger or despair when adversity hits. It does not have to be so.

One significant belief that worsens our experience of suffering is the belief that our suffering comes from God, Who is supposed to be our loving Father. We then struggle to reconcile our view of God with the presence of suffering. Our confusion makes things that much more difficult for us. Sometimes, we are told God brought our suffering to strengthen us or punish us. At other times, suffering is described as God testing our faith. We are informed our suffering must be God's will, and therefore, it must serve a greater purpose that we can't see, such as preparing us to help others who are suffering in the same way, or using us to lead others to Christ.

But what if we told you the things that bring suffering do not come from God? What if it is not a "test" or a "punishment?" What if it is not some form of twisted "lesson" for us to learn? Would that be a relief?

Adversity is the unfortunate consequence of the presence of sin in this world, and we all must endure it in one form or another, but not because God desires for us to suffer. His will for us includes peace beyond our understanding, love in the fullness of His expression of it, and an abundance of joy. Yet, God's will is not always done on earth as it is in heaven. This truth is the reason Jesus taught us to pray for God's will to be done; otherwise, that prayer has no meaning, and no reason to be included in His instruction on prayer. Our present reality is we are in this world as soldiers fighting behind enemy lines, fighting the battle against evil, and fighting against the enemy to usher in God's Kingdom. Adversity is the cost of restoring His Kingdom to a fallen world.

In the face of impending adversity, or after it sweeps through our lives, we may struggle to remain focused on the truth we know from the Lord. If we lose sight of His truth, particularly knowing Who God is and who He says we are, we lose our connection to God's peace, and suffering seems to outweigh His glory in us, rather than the other way around. We will also fail to look for and recognize His redemption, accepting instead the enemy's interpretation of our adversity. Thus, our suffering is magnified.

One of the goals of this journey is building up your strength as a warrior of God. In support of that goal, we want to highlight important truths for you to remember about adversity, and any suffering that results. Consider the following concepts as you approach dealing with adversity:

God's character is not defined by our adversity and suffering. "Jesus Christ is the same yesterday and today and forever." (Hebrews 13:8). His character and nature are revealed in His choices made on our behalf: His willingness to come as ransom for us, His suffering for us on the cross, and His resurrection. These very actions demonstrate that God opposes suffering in our lives, as He took on our shame and was wounded for our transgressions so we would not have to remain in shame and receive the punishment for our sin. He weeps over suffering with us when it comes, and redeems it when it happens, according to His identity as our

Redeemer. His love never fails. (I Corinthians 13:8). We can always know what to expect from God, even when circumstances bring the unexpected.

We are not defined by our adversity and suffering. Our identities are established by God, and are stable and secure and invariable, no matter what circumstances we go through. "You have searched me, Lord, and you know me. For you created my inmost being; you knit me together in my mother's womb" (Psalm 139:1,13). It is God Who says who we are, not the world, and not our experiences. So, during adversity and suffering, we can always go back to the truth of who we are as defined by God for our stable, unshakeable foundation on which to stand, along with the certain foundation of Who God is and how much He loves us. The Bible shares some general truths about who we are, such as identifying us as beloved children and heirs of God (I John 3:1, Romans 8:17). It is also important for us to seek from God the personal and specific answers of who He says we are. We can always rely on these unchanging truths.

Adversity does not determine our feelings. We often feel like our experiences toss us to and fro like the waves and wind, but the truth is, we choose our feelings. As we stated, our feelings during and after difficulty are based on how we perceive the adversity, and what we believe because of the difficulty, not by the difficult experience itself. Our feelings are our own, and we get to choose them. Paul admonishes us to "take captive every thought to make it obedient to Christ" (II Corinthians 10:5). The way we choose our feelings during adversity is choosing what we believe, how we think about, and how we perceive what we are experiencing. We can always seek truth from Christ to reestablish peace in our hearts, and to give us the correct interpretation of events in our lives, even during times of struggle.

Suffering is transient and temporary. When we are going through adversity, it can feel like the experience will never end, and like the worst experience we have ever had. However, the saying, "this, too, shall pass" is true of suffering. While this truth may not help much in the middle of the difficult experience, it can be a relief to know the suffering will end. Specifically related to loss, even though a loss through death is for the rest of this life, our hope remains in Jesus, that through Him our loved ones will be in heaven, everything will be restored, and we will see our loved ones again. "So we fix our eyes not on what is seen, but on what is unseen, since what is seen is temporary, but what is unseen is eternal." (II Corinthians 4:18). We can always know we are living in God's Kingdom, both now and at the end of this temporary life.

Suffering occurs in the context of my whole story. When we are suffering, we lose perspective, believing what we are going through in this moment is the worst possible experience we could ever have. Our eyes become consumed with the pain of the moment, and we lose sight of the rest of our story and the overarching story of God. However, our present experiences do have a context. The awareness that, "worse things have happened in my life" or "worse things could happen in my life," helps us to interpret suffering within the framework of the whole of our experiences, which allows us to integrate the present suffering into our whole story. Understanding our experiences through the lens of God's larger story helps us maintain perspective. "For our light and momentary troubles are achieving for us an eternal glory that far outweighs them all" (II Corinthians 4:17). We can always remember the beauty and majesty of God's story, and realize that we are an important character in His story.

Adversity will be redeemed. God is our redeemer, and as Job states: "And after my skin has been destroyed, yet in my flesh I will see God; I myself will see him with my own eyes." (Job 19:26-27). Paul describes God's redemption this way: "And we know that in all things God works for the good of those who love him, who have been called according to his purpose." (Romans 8:28). We have a Savior who knows suffering firsthand (Isaiah 53:3), so He understands where we are and what we go through. He is also the author of redemption, as His resurrection clearly demonstrates. While God does not cause suffering, He sees our suffering, and through His power and love, redeems those experiences by working in them for our good. We can always depend on the redemption of God, no matter what the difficulty, because His ultimate redemption has been demonstrated on the cross and in the empty tomb.

God is with us in our suffering. God never leaves our side. "God is our refuge and strength, an ever-present help in trouble." (Psalm 46:1). He will never leave us or forsake us (Deuteronomy 31:6, Hebrews 13:5). Just as Jesus did when He stood outside Jerusalem and wept for His children, or when He stood outside the tomb of Lazarus and wept in grief over the impact of death, He weeps with us. Throughout our experiences, He stands with us, holding us up, carrying us, and helping us. We can take heart in knowing that we are never alone. We can always know God is present with us in our suffering, and His presence brings peace and comfort, and even joy.

Adversity may be an integral part of our stories, but it does not get to write the ending and it does not determine our identities, our relationship with God, our feelings, or our future. Out of great suffering can come tremendous growth, maturation, character, perseverance, and hope – if we walk through the experience of suffering with God. Paul puts it so well: "we also glory in our sufferings, because we know that suffering produces perseverance; perseverance, character; and character, hope. And hope does not put us to shame, because God's love has been poured out into our hearts through the Holy Spirit" (Romans 5:3-5). The love of God for us, experienced deeply within our hearts, consuming our thoughts, and filling our lives, is the ever-present truth that outweighs suffering, and the force that overcomes adversity.

Questions for Prayer

Now, we seek to understand more clearly the meaning and sources of adversity and suffering by asking the Lord for truth and listening for His responses to our questions. Our questions will explore the ideas presented in this section to insure their reliability, and will open us up to receive more truth that will aide us in standing firm. Remember, if you do not readily hear from the Lord, be patient with yourself and the process. Do not push to the point of frustration; extend yourself grace, take a break from listening when needed, move on from questions where you are getting stuck, and come back to those questions later.

Be sure to use your notebook to write down responses you receive from the Lord as you pray over each question. Don't trust your memory alone to retain every detail of what He shows you.

Lord, I ask that You would be with me as I seek to listen to Your voice and learn more about suffering and adversity. Open my heart to receive Your truth, and guard my heart against the enemy's lies. Show me, Jesus...

1. In what ways have I confused suffering and adversity, believing they were one and the same?

2. What are the true sources of suffering in this world?

3. In what ways does suffering produce good fruit in my life, and what is that fruit, as You see it?

4. Is my suffering a punishment, a "test" of my faith, or a lesson set up by You?

5. Is suffering Your will?

6. How have I allowed my experiences of suffering and adversity to impact my understanding of Your character?

7. Who do You say I am?

8. Where were You when I was going through (ask about some specific personal incident of adversity)?

9. What are some examples in my life of Your redemption of my suffering?

10. Is there anything that can separate me from You, or cause You to leave me?

Meditations

Spend time contemplating the ideas presented below, always keeping your heart and mind open to the leading of the Lord. Refer to the Scriptures at the beginning of this section as you meditate on these truths. If you have questions about any of these concepts, turn to the Lord in prayer and ask Him for His understanding.

I get to choose my experience of suffering during adversity. I am able to rejoice in suffering and see the glory of Your Kingdom revealed, because I see the adversity through the lens of truth, and believe what You say about it.

Hope is found in suffering because of Your presence with me in my suffering. You strengthen me and help me to persevere, and you build my character in the process.

Your love for me pours out in my heart to push back the enemy's efforts against me. Your peace guards my heart and mind, and keeps my thoughts aligned with Your thoughts.

I know You are someone acquainted with suffering, so You understand my experience. You showed me in Gethsemane what it looks like to face adversity through relationship with the Father, and You demonstrated on the cross how peace and glory can reign, even in great suffering.

Your resurrection proves Your redemption will always come; the enemy will not defeat me with You living within me.

Process

Process these suggested areas of focus based on this section. Remember, the goal is for you to grasp concepts, not develop a list of steps to take or rules to follow. If you understand the concepts, you will be able to see the whole picture, and can better understand any of its parts and apply the information presented to your own life. These suggestions may not match concepts that you valued from this section, so add your own concepts, based on beliefs and attitudes you have chosen to adopt from the reading and your time with the Lord, and applications that work for you. Incorporate these concepts in your daily meditations and prayer. As you synthesize and apply these concepts, combine them with the concepts you learned in the first section. Practice recalling each concept during times of adversity, and applying the concepts, with the Lord's help.

Synthesis: Rather than interpreting suffering on my own, I choose to allow Your truth to determine my beliefs, and Your peace to guard my heart and mind.

Application: When I suffer:

I will go to a quiet place, away from distractions and stimulation.

I will consider the larger context of the suffering within my whole story.

I will reject any thoughts, beliefs, or perceptions that do not agree with truth.

I will repeat whatever truth I receive from the Lord several times throughout my experience of adversity.

Synthesis: I choose to look for Your redemption during and after any experience of adversity. Instead of focusing on the circumstances, I choose to fix my eyes on You.

Application: When I come through adversity:

I will intentionally turn my attention toward the Lord and away from the circumstances.

I will ask the Lord for His love to fill, restore, and comfort my heart.

I will ask for eyes to see the Lord's redemption of my circumstances.

I will continue to look for the Lord's redemption until He reveals it.

I will identify His redemption for what it is, and offer my thanks for it when it comes.

Conclusion

In Section Two, we discussed the definitions of adversity and suffering, and learned how they were different, but connected. Adversity is hardship, something opposing us, originating from the enemy. Suffering is our emotional and physiological experience through the adversity, originating from our own beliefs and perceptions. We encourage you to practice taking your thoughts captive by turning to Jesus to receive truth at the onset of any adversity, allowing that truth to direct your beliefs and perceptions, and so influence your experience of suffering. As you walk through the Valley, listen for the truth from Jesus, and focus on His presence in your heart. As you brave the Storm, allow His love to envelope you and His peace to surround you like a shield. His love outweighs anything adversity could throw at you.

Now, let's learn about the goals and objectives of the enemy. As warriors fighting behind enemy lines, we need to be the best prepared soldiers of all. Understanding the adversary's plans will help prepare us to stand.

STRENGTH IN ADVERSITY

THREE

IDENTIFY THE SOURCE

Scripture

Remember to take time to read each verse carefully and in depth, not by rote, and to consider their application to facing adversity. Look up each verse, and read several verses leading up to and following the selection to understand the context. Ask what the Lord is wanting to say to you as you read these verses.

Genesis 3:1-5, 7-8 Now the serpent was more crafty than any of the wild animals the LORD God had made. He said to the woman, "Did God really say, 'You must not eat from any tree in the garden'?" The woman said to the serpent, "We may eat fruit from the trees in the garden, but God did say, 'You must not eat fruit from the tree that is in the middle of the garden, and you must not touch it, or you will die.'" "You will not certainly die," the serpent said to the woman. "For God knows that when you eat from it your eyes will be opened, and you will be like God, knowing good and evil." They realized they were naked; so, they sewed fig leaves together and made coverings for themselves. Then the man and his wife heard the sound of the LORD God as he was walking in the garden in the cool of the day, and they hid from the L<small>ORD</small> *God among the trees of the garden.*

John 10:10 *The thief comes only to steal and kill and destroy; I have come that they may have life, and have it to the full.*

Matthew 13:19 *When anyone hears the message about the kingdom and does not understand it, the evil one comes and snatches away what was sown in their heart.*

Mark 3:24-25 *If a kingdom is divided against itself, that kingdom cannot stand. If a house is divided against itself, that house cannot stand.*

Ephesians 6:10-12 *Finally, be strong in the Lord and in his mighty power. Put on the full armor of God, so that you can take your stand against the devil's schemes. For our struggle is not against flesh and blood, but against the rulers, against the authorities, against the powers of this dark world and against the spiritual forces of evil in the heavenly realms.*

Enemy Objectives

Because we look around us with worldly eyes, we don't see our actual condition. We have relative ease and comfort and security in the worldly sense, so to us, any discomfort, difficulty, or threat to worldly security equates to suffering. However, our reality, if we had the eyes to see it, is we are standing in the middle of a pitched battle, an intense struggle of a very different kind. We are at war.

Our enemies are the "powers of this dark world" and "the spiritual forces of evil in the heavenly realms" (Ephesians 6:12). Before us and all around us, the forces of the enemy are arrayed, armed with cunning, skilled at deception, and empowered with usurped authority, and we wander into their hands like blind sheep to the slaughter. "Hear, you deaf; look, you blind, and see! You have seen many things, but you pay no attention; your ears are open, but you do not listen…this is a people plundered and looted, all of them trapped in pits or hidden away in prisons. They have become plunder" (Isaiah 42:18, 20, 22).

If we really saw the perilous environment we live in, we would behave like soldiers behave when they are on the front lines. We would train and prepare as if our lives depended on it; we would care for our weapons like precious treasures; we would have our fellow soldiers' backs always; we would remain on constant guard over our territory. Our preparation, discipline, and diligence would be a matter of life and death. How many Christians do you know who live this way?

Because we are ill-prepared, we become "a people plundered and looted" by the enemy. We are "trapped in pits" of his lies and "hidden away in prisons" of our own design. The joy of the Lord is sucked away, so our strength is gone (Nehemiah 8:10). We can't stand in the face of worldly adversity, much less the deadlier snares of Satan.

To adequately prepare, we need to know what our weapons are and what weapons are being used against us. We need to understand the goals of our enemy, anticipating the kinds of attacks coming our way. We need to recognize Satan's objectives, to know what to protect against and how to defend against him. And we need to train, based on this information, so we are ready when the attacks come. In preparation for strengthening you to stand in adversity, this section will present the goals and objectives of the enemy, and will begin to explore our weapons provided by God for our defense.

First, we need to understand the primary goals of the enemy. The two goals are actually very simple. Satan seeks to cover up or hide our true nature in Christ, to keep us from being fully who God created us to be, so that our God-given identity doesn't flow freely into the world. Satan knows accomplishing this goal hinders God's love from flowing out of us to others, thus limiting the experience of His Kingdom in this world, allowing the enemy to maintain his status as "ruler of the kingdom of the air" (Ephesians 2:2).

Satan's second goal is to leave us with the impression we have no choices. The enemy doesn't have the power to remove our freedom to choose, which is God-ordained, so he deceives us into believing our choices are limited or nonexistent, which is just as effective. Because freedom to choose is required for love to be given and received, getting us to believe we have few or no choices limits our ability to give and receive love, which is, of course, the very nature of God, and His two primary commandments. This goal restricts us from experiencing the flow of God's love in our hearts, even though His love continues to pour out, freely given to us.

To accomplish these two goals, Satan uses his only weapon: deception. Something interesting to note about deception is, it is only effective if we believe it. In other words, the enemy's sole weapon only works with our agreement and participation. This truth would be liberating, if we were not so consumed in the enemy's lies, because it means Satan can't do anything to us if we don't let him. It is also the reason the truth is such a powerful weapon in our arsenal.

The enemy uses three lies to weave "a cord of three strands" which is not easily broken (Ecclesiastes 4:12). In Genesis 3, we see the three lies being played out, to the detriment of all mankind. Satan's first lie, his contention that we can "be like God" (Genesis 3:5), leaves us believing we are god and judge over our own lives, so we try to assume control and we judge ourselves and others. As it says in James 2:4, "have you not discriminated among yourselves and become judges with evil thoughts?" From this root lie grows two more lies: shame and fear.

Satan begins as early as possible planting seeds of fear and shame in us to gain increasing amounts of authority in our lives, usurped from the authority given to us by God in His gift of free will. Our freedom to choose is increasingly stolen by the enemy as we relinquish our freedom in exchange for a false promise of safety from whatever we fear, and a hiding place to cover up whatever shames us. His objective is to deceive us into believing in the illusion of control, which enables him to drive us like a horse under his whip, while our eyes see only our own feet on the road and our own head setting off in a direction. All the while, the enemy is steering us through fear and shame toward his desired results.

The only way to be truly free, paradoxically, is to surrender to Christ, for "perfect love drives out fear, because fear has to do with punishment" (I John 4:18), and "anyone who believes in Him will never be put to shame" (Romans 10:11). If we willingly let go of the illusion of control, which feels to us like we are giving up control but is actually severing our agreement with the enemy in fear and shame, we regain our freedom and take back our authority in Christ that Satan usurped. Where Satan increasingly limits our choices, Jesus offers us grace to cover our sin, removing our fear and shame, and infinite choices, restoring our freedom. To gain our lives, we must lose our lives. When we lose our lives to Christ, only then will we find true life.

Another of Satan's objectives is division. He wants us to experience division on multiple levels, but his primary target is to promote the illusion of division from God. As we have seen with the illusion of control, he once again uses shame and fear to generate this illusion of separation from God. Paul tells us nothing can separate us from the love of God in Christ (Romans 8:38-39), but the enemy attempts to convince us that our sin divides us from God's love. In truth, our feelings of and belief in shame create the illusion of division from God, as we cover our eyes and cover our sin, thus giving us the feeling of separation. Then, just like Adam and Eve, we run from God and hide in fear of His judgment, not remembering that perfect love drives out fear. So, we are left feeling divided from God. We see Him as "up there" or "far away" and begin to believe we must be "good enough" to earn His love. Do you hear the self-judgment in that statement?

In addition to division from God, Satan wants to create internal division within us. Fundamentally, he wants us to close off who we are, and live instead from a false identity, a mask of sorts that he convinces us will be pleasing to the world, or even to God. As we have explained, when we cover up our God-given nature, which expresses some aspect of God's nature that He has gifted within us at our creation, our true self is not allowed to flow freely into the world, thus hindering the full experience of God's Kingdom. If we live long enough from a false identity, the mask starts feeling real to us, and we forget who we really are. Our hearts and minds become divided, and we are "double-minded and unstable" in our ways (James 1:8).

Finally, Satan seeks to create division between ourselves and others. Paul warns explicitly against division within the church (I

Corinthians 1:10, 11:18, 12:25) and he cautions to stay away from those who cause divisions in the body of Christ, just as one would stay away from evil (Romans 16:17). If we look at the church today, we can see how successful Satan has been in achieving this objective. However, relational division is not only apparent in the church. Our culture is rife with division: rich vs. poor, black vs. white, conservative vs. liberal, secular vs. religious, and the list goes on and on. What is the source of these many divisions? The answer is fear, because most of the cultural divisions listed here are based in the illusion of control.

Since love of God and love of neighbor are the commandments which sum up all of Scripture, is it surprising the enemy of God would promote division on every level? Love is our most powerful weapon against division. Satan uses the lies of judgment, fear, and shame to suppress love, because he knows, as the cross demonstrated, love is the ultimate weapon that defeats evil.

To accomplish his objectives and meet his goals, Satan entices us in two directions. First, he tries to allure us with a hiding place, a Cave of his design, but all along he claims it benefits us, either by providing a place of safety and security where he claims we won't be hurt anymore, or by providing a place to hide our shame from the sight of others which he claims protects our self-image. He makes the hiding place look appealing and desirable; however, what is hidden from us is the true nature of our prison.

Once we step inside his prison, we are in his territory, and, therefore, engulfed in a personal, torturous, private hell, where Satan's minions can send the full force of their onslaught against our minds, with no limitations or restrictions. At the same time, Satan accuses us before God, claiming we chose to be there of our own free will, effectively giving the enemy full permission to do whatever he wants with us.

Satan also entices us to desire control. He manipulates us into giving away our true authority, then convinces us power over others, ourselves, and circumstances is the solution to this loss of our authority. Of course, he is sure to fan our powerless and trapped beliefs and feelings to get us to buy into trying to control. What he doesn't tell us is the more we try to control, the more he can feed those same out of control feelings, which he continues until we are paralyzed by fear, convinced we are abject failures, and despising who we are.

We can learn about our enemy from the things we observe him doing. For example, we can clearly see he is not creative. His goals never change and he uses the same limited devices repeatedly. He is bound to the story written about him in Scripture, and can do nothing except play it out. Unlike our enemy, we have been imbued with the creative spark of our Creator God. Our stories are written in partnership with our Creator. We can imagine different storylines, and if we can imagine a new story, we can create it.

We can also see how Satan has no power over us. He needs us to believe him, and agree to come into his Cave or to take the reins of control before he can do anything more to us. He is limited by our freedom to choose, which he cannot subvert because it is God-ordained.

Finally, we can observe how Satan always withholds the most crucial information from us, while giving the appearance of offering something that we think we want. He can't change the truth; he can only try to hide it from us or present a perverted or distorted view of it, hoping we will accept his view. If we ask Jesus to bring light to whatever Satan is trying to convince us to accept, the actual nature of his hiding place and the true results of control will be revealed.

Now, understanding Satan's two goals, his three basic lies, and his primary objectives, we can begin to identify the source of our thoughts. Each of our thoughts reflect one kingdom or the other; in other words, they are either of God or of the enemy. Beliefs determine feelings, so guarding our thoughts and keeping them focused on truth is our primary line of defense. Once we can discern the source of our thoughts, we know which thoughts to accept and which to reject. We can recognize lie beliefs, and seek the truth from the Lord to replace any lies that come up in our hearts and minds.

Most of the time, we simply accept whatever thoughts arise in our minds as our own, and, without consideration, we feel they are true. However, since we are soldiers, we cannot afford to be lazy or ineffective in guarding our thoughts. This process requires immediate screening and evaluation. First, we identify the source. Is the thought of the Kingdom of God, or is it an enemy thought, and lie-based?

Think of your mind as the living room in your house. If someone knocks on your door to enter, don't you usually check to see who is knocking before opening the door? At the very least, you stop a visitor at the door to see who it is before you let them come barging into your living room. The evaluation and screening of your thoughts needs to occur before you let them in your mental living room.

Pretend you have the equivalent of a foyer or a mud room at your mental front door. If you are not certain the source of the thought, and you let it in to evaluate it, keep the thought in the mud room/foyer while you check it out. Don't internalize the thought or receive the thought in your heart until you have had the opportunity to evaluate its source.

Slam your mental door on any judgments of self or others. Judgment here does not refer to discerning good from evil, or right from wrong, which we are supposed to do, according to Scripture; for example, recognizing a thought as a lie is the form of judgment that recognizes righteousness. We are called to use good judgment based on wisdom when making choices. The judgment of self or others described here is related to hierarchical division and condemnation.

These self-as-god judgments may sound like these types of thoughts: "I don't matter;" "I'll never be good enough;" "I'm not loved, or wanted;" "I'm worthless;" and the same kinds of expressions directed toward someone else, such as, "he or she doesn't matter; "he or she is not worthy;" etc. Remember, these judgments will *feel* true to you, so you don't want to accept a thought based on your feelings. Instead, use your feelings to help identify the lie. Does the thought bring a feeling of peace, or joy? Does the thought express love? If so, the thought is of God's Kingdom. Feelings of debasement, discouragement, hopelessness, despair, bitterness, and loathing are of the enemy.

Close the door also on fear and shame. You can recognize fear-based lies in the phrases, "have to," "can't," "must," and "what if?" Shame-based lies bring condemnation, and include "should," "shouldn't," "ought to," "ought not," "I'm/you're bad," and "my/your fault." Like the judgments, these lies will *feel* true to you, so listen to your inner language and word choices, and evaluate the source based on language instead of feelings. If unsure of the source, check for what the beliefs produce in you. You will know them by their fruit (Matthew 7:16).

If you find yourself in any of the places we use to identify types of adversity: from the bondage of Egypt to the isolation of a self-imposed hiding place; from walking through your own fire to the emptiness of lack; from the Wilderness of desires just out of reach to the Storm of chaos and doubt; from the Valley of illness to the Tomb of grief; look first to your beliefs. See if you are believing in judgments, in fear, or in shame. No matter your circumstances, if you return your beliefs to the truth of Christ, your experience of the battle will also change.

Jesus offers truth replacements for each of the three enemy lies. In the place of judgment, open your door to the revelation of your true identity in Christ, and live in the fullness of who He created you to be. In the place of fear, open your door to the concept of choice. We do not have control, but based on the gift of free will, we always have a choice, and even when we choose poorly, we can always choose differently or choose to make it right. In the place of shame, open your door to taking responsibility, which means accepting that our choices produce certain consequences. Unlike shame, which condemns us as bad and sucks us like quicksand down into despair, taking responsibility empowers us to make new and different choices. Combined, these truths restore our freedom, and "it is for freedom that Christ has set us free." (Galatians 5:1).

Questions for Prayer

Now, we seek to recognize the goals and objectives of the enemy, and correctly identify the source of our thoughts by asking the Lord for truth and listening for His responses to our questions. Our questions will explore the ideas presented in this section to insure their reliability, and will open us up to receive more truth that will develop our discernment. Remember, if you do not readily hear from the Lord, be patient with yourself and the process. Do not push to the point of frustration; extend yourself grace, take a break from listening when needed, move on from questions where you are getting stuck, and come back to those questions later.

Be sure to use your notebook to write down responses you receive from the Lord as you pray over each question. Don't trust your memory alone to retain every detail of what He shows you.

Lord, I ask that You would be with me as I seek to listen to Your voice and learn more about fighting the adversary. Open my heart to receive Your truth, and guard my heart against the enemy's lies. Show me, Jesus…

1. What does it mean to be a soldier in a war for Your Kingdom?

2. In my life, how has Satan usurped Your authority and plundered my joy and peace?

3. How do I use truth and love to fight the enemy?

4. In what ways have I believed in the illusion of control?

5. What is my true identity, and how is my true identity hidden from me and from others?

6. Where has Satan attempted to limit my choices?

7. In my life, where has division taken hold?

8. What judgments have I made against myself and others?

9. What fear-based lies am I believing?

10. What shame-based lies am I believing?

Meditations

Spend time contemplating the ideas presented below, always keeping your heart and mind open to the leading of the Lord. Refer to the Scriptures at the beginning of this section as you meditate on these truths. If you have questions about any of these concepts, turn to the Lord in prayer and ask Him for His understanding.

I am Your soldier, fighting a pitched battle against a cunning and deceptive adversary whose forces surround me, but You live in my heart, which gives me the distinct advantages of authority, and freedom. If I choose to believe Your truth, the enemy is completely powerless against me.

While Satan seeks to convince me to judge and control, and his deceptions feel enticing because they claim to offer me safety and security, You offer me unconditional love. Because of Your love, I have nothing to fear.

Satan tries to create division within me by tempting me to hide my true nature; the illusion of division from You by tempting me to believe I am bad, unloved, and unworthy; and, division from

Your children whom You love dearly, as You love me, isolating me to make me easier prey.

The root of self as god and its accompanying judgments goes all the way back to Adam and Eve. This root lie produces the fruit of fear and shame, which directly oppose love and freedom, and bind me in the enemy's traps. Freedom from these snares comes from completely surrendering my life to You.

Your gift of free will says I always have a choice, no matter my circumstances. With Your help, I can identify the source of my thoughts, and I can always choose which voice I will listen to and which Kingdom way I will follow.

Process

Process these suggested areas of focus based on this section. Remember, the goal is for you to grasp concepts, not develop a list of steps to take or rules to follow. If you understand the concepts, you will be able to see the whole picture, and can better understand any of its parts and apply the information presented to your own life. These suggestions may not match concepts that you valued from this section, so add your own concepts, based on beliefs and attitudes you have chosen to adopt from the reading and your time with the Lord, and applications that work for you. Incorporate these concepts in your daily meditations and prayer. As you synthesize and apply these concepts, combine them with the concepts you learned in the first two sections. Practice recalling each concept during times of adversity, and applying the concepts, with the Lord's help.

Synthesis: Rather than immediately accepting thoughts I have as true and my own, I choose to evaluate and identify the source of my thoughts as either of Your Kingdom or of the enemy, and not allow any thoughts to inhabit my mind that are not of Your Kingdom.

Application: When thoughts come:

I will examine the thought against known truth I have received from the Lord or learned through Scripture.

I will listen for the language of judgment, fear, and shame.

I will check what feelings the thought produces, and measure those feelings against love, peace, and joy.

I will envision myself closing the door on any thought that does not match known truth; includes the language of judgment, fear, or shame; and/or, produces feelings not of the fruit of the Spirit.

I will envision myself inviting in and welcoming any thought I identify as of God's Kingdom.

Synthesis: I choose to exercise the authority and freedom You have given me by choosing to surrender my life to You.

Application: When I judge or attempt to control:

I will humble myself and admit to the Lord that I am not God over my life.

I will repent (turn from) attempting to control or acting as judge.

I will meditate on the Lord's love for me, reviewing specific memories and examples of His care and loving action on my behalf, including the cross.

I will offer whatever I am attempting to control into the Lord's hands, and relinquish the outcome to His care.

I will replace judgments of myself with truth based on who the Lord says I am, and judgments of others by asking the Lord how He sees the person I am judging.

Conclusion

In Section Three, we discussed the importance of preparation and awareness of our enemy's goals because we are at war. We identified the enemy's two main goals as covering or hiding who we are, and limiting our choices. Satan uses the three lies of self-as-god, fear, and shame to usurp our authority, to entice us to try to control, and to create division. We encourage you to practice identifying the source of your thoughts, and closing the door on any thoughts that are of the enemy, while welcoming and embracing thoughts that are of God's Kingdom. As you walk through the Valley, recognize the source of your hardship, listen for the truth from Jesus, and focus on His presence in your heart. As you brave the Storm, allow His love to envelope you and His peace to surround you like a shield. His love is a more powerful weapon than anything Satan could throw at you.

Now, let's learn about the strategies of the enemy. As warriors fighting behind enemy lines, we need to be the best prepared soldiers of all. Anticipating the adversary's tactics will help prepare us to stand.

STRENGTH IN ADVERSITY

FOUR

RESIST

Scripture

Remember to take time to read each verse carefully and in depth, not by rote, and to consider their application to facing adversity. Look up each verse, and read several verses leading up to and following the selection to understand the context. Ask what the Lord is wanting to say to you as you read these verses.

Matthew 10:16 *"I am sending you out like sheep among wolves. Therefore, be as shrewd as snakes and as innocent as doves."*

I Peter 5:8-9 *Be alert and of sober mind. Your enemy the devil prowls around like a roaring lion looking for someone to devour. Resist him, standing firm in the faith.*

II Corinthians 2:10-11 *Anyone you forgive, I also forgive. And what I have forgiven—if there was anything to forgive—I have forgiven in the sight of Christ for your sake, in order that Satan might not outwit us. For we are not unaware of his schemes.*

James 4:7 *Submit yourselves, then, to God. Resist the devil, and he will flee from you.*

Romans 12:21 *Do not be overcome by evil, but overcome evil with good.*

I Corinthians 14:20 *In regard to evil be infants, but in your thinking be adults.*

II Thessalonians 3:3 *But the Lord is faithful, and he will strengthen you and protect you from the evil one.*

Enemy Tactics

Satan is very cunning. He rarely comes after us with overt and obvious assaults, at least not until he already has us thoroughly confused and reeling. Often, he comes at us in inches and degrees. He is skilled at taking a truth and twisting it one degree off center, distorting or perverting it just enough so that it is no longer true, but still sounds plausible, or even factual. We see an example of this in Scripture when Satan tempted Jesus in the wilderness. Satan quoted actual Scripture to support his position; however, he had distorted the meaning of the Scriptural quote, and applied it, not as it was intended or as it was presented in context, but to tempt Jesus to test God (Matthew 4:5-7). Jesus responded, as He did to each temptation, with truth.

Satan's desire was to subvert Jesus' mission, and that is still his desire, but now he is focused on tricking us into helping him accomplish his goal and fulfill his desire. What better way to undermine the gospel than to pervert Scripture just enough that it loses its power, dissuades us from the truth, and leaves us with doubt in the trustworthiness and goodness of God? Haven't we all witnessed or experienced the misuse of Scripture to either condemn or to justify mistreatment of another? How often is Scripture perverted in such a way that individuals' hearts are wounded by it rather than healed? This is the work of the enemy, not of God!

Satan's machinations are a quagmire of pitfalls, trip wires, and enticements, many of which sound good to us, and even "Christian-y," and most of which feel true to us at the time. With Satan being so skilled at twisting truth and manipulating us, and with our limitations in being able to clearly identify truth from lie, how can we ever hope to navigate through life and remain in the truth of Christ?

The answer is that, on our own, we absolutely cannot. We will be tripped up. We will be trapped. We will be deceived. We will be tempted. The original lie that we can be our own god is engraved on our soul in much the same way that our eye color is written into our DNA. Before we are cognitively able to understand what we are doing, we are already saying "no" and "mine." One glance at another person, and a judgment has been made before we even have the chance to think about it, and we are instantaneously condemned. Can you see why the enemy's lie of shame is so insidious and destructive? According to him, we are shameful before we even start, and at fault for something that was not our choice. How can we ever escape such a vicious snare, when we are so impossibly entangled? We can't manage it.

Fortunately, we are not on our own. Through the presence of Jesus in our hearts, and by listening to His Spirit, we can have those pitfalls brought to light. We can hear the truth at the time when the deception is calling us into a trap. Even when we trip up, which we will, we can be caught in God's loving arms before we fall into Satan's pit. We can take responsibility for what we choose instead of feeling shame for what we did not choose.

Rather than focus on our own efforts such that we feel it is hopeless and we end up defeated, we can focus our heart and mind on Jesus. We can ask for truth at each turn of our path, and at each presentation of something that is not of God, and absorb His truth like we would melt into the warmth of soothing water. The more we allow His truth to permeate our thoughts and our feelings, the closer our connection with Jesus feels and the more peace we receive, and the less the enemy ensnares us.

Continuing your preparation for standing in adversity, this section will present some of the fundamental strategies and tactics the enemy uses against you, because forewarned is forearmed. At the same time, you will continue to explore how God strengthens you, prepares you, and defends you in the battle.

Games Satan plays. Let's begin by exploring some of the games of the enemy. It is important to recognize this element of game-playing as something of the enemy that is both distinctive from God and contrary to God's nature. Paul put it this way: "What harmony is there between Christ and Belial?" (II Corinthians 6:15). As we indicated, Satan is cunning, calculating, and manipulative. He has a strategy that he follows, and a set of so-called "rules" that he adheres to in some form or fashion in his gamesmanship that are very legalistic, although he is always looking for loopholes.

He deceives as his singular move in his games. Of course, he tries to deceive in a wide variety of ways, but at its base, his strategy involves lying, and his lies are basically predictable. It sounds simple, doesn't it? Just recognize the lies! What makes it seem so difficult to win against, for us, is that he is really good at lying, and he couches his lies in things that feel true in our hearts, while using distorted perceptions of our experiences to give us proof text that his lies are true. He wraps his lies in complicated and confusing partial truths and distortions, leaving us uncertain what to believe or even who to believe.

He offers us "gifts" of things our flesh craves, such as momentary gratification, an illusion of safety or security, a hiding place to cover our sin and shame, and a reinforcement of our own sense of being god over our lives, in exchange for binding ourselves to him in a covenant arrangement that gives him authority to influence our thoughts and feelings, and obligates us to agree with his perverse views of ourselves, God, and life. Then, he consistently "rewards" our agreement with him by reinforcing our need for his gifts.

Satan is like the malicious stranger in the nondescript sedan, dangling candy out the window to entice us into his car. He wants us to play the role of the naïve child walking home from school, who doesn't know any better than to take candy from a stranger. He makes the candy seem very appealing to the eye and enticing in what he purports that it provides us, so we want it. (Remember the Israelites wanting to return to slavery in Egypt? – Exodus 17:3) If we get in the car and take the candy, we will taste sweetness, but just for a moment. The candy then turns bitter in our mouths and the bitterness is so awful, we become desperate for something to take that bitter taste away. But now, we are kidnapped and in the enemy's car, and our choices seem limited to us.

Of course, Satan is ready and offers another piece of candy, and the momentary sweetness brings what feels to us like relief. But the relief is short-lived, and our desperation grows as the bitterness deepens. We soon believe his candy is the only thing that can help us, and the only thing we need. Anything seems better than that bitter taste. We are blinded to the fact that it was Satan's candy that produced the bitterness in the first place.

All of Satan's gifts turn bitter, as Scripture warns. "Though evil is sweet in his mouth and he hides it under his tongue, though he cannot bear to let it go and keeps it in his mouth, yet his food will turn sour in his stomach, it will become the venom of serpents within him" (Job 20:12-14). If we acknowledge our need for Jesus and resist the urge to keep taking Satan's candy, He promises to restore us and lift us up. The sweetness of Jesus is beyond anything we have ever experienced, so superior to the enemy's brief moment of so-called relief that we will wonder why we were ever enticed by the candy to begin with. Nothing compares to His love. Nothing is sweeter than His truth. "How sweet are your words to my taste, sweeter than honey to my mouth!" (Psalm 119:103).

Let's look at some other strategies the enemy uses. For example, his own whispers condemn us, then he turns around and reminds us that because of our shame, we need his hiding place, and isn't he wonderful for providing us a (self-made) prison to hide in? (Remember the Cave where David hid from Saul? – Psalm 57:1) When, after a while, we complain about the prison and seek release, he shrugs his shoulders and reminds us we chose to construct it and we chose to go there, shaming us once again. Soon, we see no way out of the prison we are in.

He deceives us into sinning by telling us it will feel good in the moment, then turns around and condemns us for doing it. Quickly on the heels of his condemnation, he reminds us if we would just do the sin behavior again, we would feel better. (Remember the temptations the enemy spoke to Jesus in the Desert? – Matthew 4:3, 6, 9)

He emboldens us with exaggerated praise and self-aggrandizement, telling us who we are is what we accomplish or produce, and we take off running after some external goal as proof of our value. Shortly after, he whispers his constant reminder that we are bound to fail, and fear grips us. We then begin to create what we most fear. When we do inevitably fail, since we are not God, he is Johnny-on-the-spot to shame us for failing and demolish our fragile sense of who we are. (Remember the Israelites' failure to face the giants in the land, and how it left them wandering in the Wilderness? – Psalm 106:24-26)

So, basically, Satan is running a game of three-card Monte. He selects his cards from a limited deck (fear, shame, and self-as-god), but like the sneak he is, he gives us the appearance of having virtually all the cards in his hand. He will even show us his cards, and, if we pay attention as he plays his hand, we can figure out what his next move will likely be. It just doesn't make that move any less effective against us, because we have so deeply bought into his system, he has convinced us we can win at his game. As a result, we continue to play Satan's game by Satan's rules.

In truth, we have three God-cards to beat Satan, because God's cards trump Satan's self-as-god, fear, and shame, and we can play them as often and as many times as we want. God's cards are simple truths, and His hand is played openly and aboveboard.

Card one, played against Satan's self-as-god card, is humility. The definition of humility is, "God is God, and I am not." While Satan would pervert humility into self-debasement, a form of self-judgment, thus turning it into one of his three cards, God calls us His children and heirs, a position of incredible honor which at the same time acknowledges God is indeed God.

Card two, played against the shame card of the enemy, is the cross. What can Satan do or say against that ultimate trump card? Our sin is completely covered, death is rendered powerless, and our value and worth to God is proven.

Card three, played against Satan's fear card, is reaffirmed by our first two God-cards: God's love for us. His perfect love casts out all fear. The root of all our fears is the fear of death, but the resurrection of Christ has defeated death of any kind once and for all. Death of ourselves, in one form or another, is why we crave Satan's so-called safety and security, and are willing to sell ourselves out for the illusion he offers. Jesus' willingness to take on that battle against the wages of our sin for us demonstrates just how far He is willing to go on our behalf. Nothing is beyond the reach of this card.

These cards trump any card Satan might play, no matter how skillfully he tries to play them. If we play our cards right, Satan can do nothing and his defeat is already certain.

Now, in contrast to the enemy, God does not play bait-and-switch games with our lives. His cards are on the table. He doesn't manipulate us, he doesn't control us, and he doesn't calculate how to use us. Instead, He partners with us so we "may participate in the divine nature" (II Peter 1:4). While He provides us weapons to use against His enemy, He would never use us as "pawns" in the enemy's game. Just like He called Moses to go before Pharaoh as God's partner, David to stand before Goliath as God's partner, and Shadrach, Meshach, and Abednego to stand before Nebuchadnezzar as God's partner, He calls us to stand against the enemy as God's partner, demonstrating to us our value and worth, and confirming for us the importance of our participation and our freedom to choose to walk with Him.

While Satan plays us, God loves us, shares with us, and empowers us. Unlike Satan, who doesn't care which of us he uses or how he uses us, since he only cares about hurting God, God creates each one of us uniquely, fearfully and wonderfully made as His children (Psalm 139:14). We are beautiful reflections of the Father, who, simply by being who He created us to be, shine the light of God into the darkness of the world, bringing the Kingdom on earth, each in a unique way that only we can usher in. In other words, our unique and special presence matters to God simply for who we are.

What a stark contrast to Satan, the slimy game-player! God knows us, He sees us, and He deeply loves us – as the cross speaks in action – and He desires us – as His choice to give us the freedom to choose Him out of love shows us. Truly, "if God is for us, who can be against us?" (Romans 8:31).

Satan the dirty player. In football, when a defensive player tackles the opposing runner with the ball, the rest of his team jumps on top to create a pile. Dirty players jump on late, when the player believes the play is over and their guard is down. Ostensibly, this technique is to insure the opposing player stays down, but the secondary, unstated gain is an increased chance of causing injury to the downed player.

Satan is like a dirty football player. When he gets us to accept one little lie, he immediately begins to pile on, interpreting circumstance after circumstance in a way to bring in other, more damaging lies, and to expand his territory in our beliefs. (Remember the three enemies allied against Israel at Berakah? – II Chronicles 20:1) He hits us late, he hits us from all sides, and he hits us hard, especially when we are vulnerable.

Satan the octopus. Satan works his tentacles over us all the time, ever seeking a little crack in our defenses, or the tiniest point of access into our hearts or minds. (Remember how Jesus was tormented at Gethsemane? – Matthew 26:38) He is relentless, persistent, and thorough, and he doesn't tire of the game. We, on the other hand, do get fatigued in the battle, and as we tire, we become more vulnerable to his attempts at access. We are doing our best to guard our front doors, and he is sneaking through a crack in a corner of our basement wall.

This strategy of the enemy highlights the vital importance of our reliance on God, for without His help, we can't hope to maintain the oversight needed to prevent Satan from finding that tiny crack. We all believe lies of some kind, so we all are vulnerable to the father of lies. He will eventually wear us down with his constant prying and worming his way in, if we do not surrender to God and depend completely on His guard over our hearts and minds (Philippians 4:7).

Satan the bully. The description of the enemy in I Peter 5:8 as prowling around "like a roaring lion looking for someone to devour" reveals that, more than anything, Satan is a bully, seeking to gather toadies around him to develop a gang. He uses intimidation, manipulation, and false promises of power or personal gain or protection to get us to join his gang. Those who refuse he attempts to destroy, or render meaningless. Those who acquiesce he uses and bleeds dry, then throws them away after they have served his purposes. Those who willingly join up he grooms into mirror reflections of himself to broaden his reach, to destroy resisters, and to recruit more members to the gang.

Everything the enemy does is about gaining power and control, indicating that, just like a bully, he actually has no power at all. Of course, this is exactly why he needs a gang. He needs us to agree with his deceptions and to follow his plans, or he cannot do his dirty work. We become his hands and feet. We are the ones who must agree to give him access to us and to others through our lies and sin, for if we refused him, and refused to believe his lies, what could he do? Everyone knows there is only one way to deal with a bully: stand up.

We were reminded of Opie, in an episode of the Andy Griffith Show, paying his milk money every morning to the school bully, and how Andy told him the story from his own childhood of dealing with a bully who was stealing his fishing hole. Andy said, "Found out that tough talk's just talk. Because it come to me that what I'd been so scared of wasn't really worth bein' scared of at all. I didn't even feel that knuckle sandwich. Not a bit. And I lit into him like a windmill in a tornado." Opie went to school the next day, refused to give up his milk money, closed his eyes and said, "I hope you was tellin' me the truth, Pa," and then later Opie tells Andy he "sailed into him like a windmill in a tornado," just like his Pa did. Opie got back his stolen money, and learned a valuable lesson in life from his father.[2]

What lessons can we learn from our Father in how to deal with the resident bully of the world? Jesus' example to us was to stand up to the bully, to beat him using real authority, and to refuse his schemes and deceptions. We have been empowered by Christ to do the same. Like Opie, if we see the enemy in the light of truth, realizing he has no real power, and that his "tough talk's just talk," we are equipped with the truth of Jesus to stand our ground.

Questions for Prayer

Now, we seek to recognize the tactics and strategies of the enemy, and prepare ourselves to resist his schemes by asking the Lord for truth and listening for His responses to our questions. Our questions will explore the ideas presented in this section to insure their reliability, and will open us up to receive more truth that will continue to strengthen our stand. Remember, if you do not readily hear from the Lord, be patient with yourself and the process. Do not push to the point of frustration; extend yourself grace, take a break from listening when needed, move on from questions where you are getting stuck, and come back to those questions later.

Be sure to use your notebook to write down responses you receive from the Lord as you pray over each question. Don't trust your memory alone to retain every detail of what He shows you.

Lord, I ask that You would be with me as I seek to listen to Your voice and learn more about fighting the adversary. Open my heart to receive Your truth, and guard my heart against the enemy's lies. Show me, Jesus...

1. What are some examples of ways I am unknowingly assisting the enemy in his desire to subvert Your mission and undermine the gospel?

2. What are some unidentified deceptions the enemy has used against me that sound true but are one degree off?

3. What "gifts" has Satan offered me that I have agreed to accept?

4. Have I made a covenant or agreement with the enemy that I am unaware I made?

5. Do I have a hiding place (prison) within my heart that needs to be exposed?

6. In what ways have I taken the bait and run after Satan's offer of value based on outcomes and production?

7. How can I use humility to trump Satan's game in my life?

8. How does the cross overcome shame in my life?

9. How does Your love overcome fear in my life?

10. What lesson would You teach me about how to stand up to Satan, the bully?

Meditations

Spend time contemplating the ideas presented below, always keeping your heart and mind open to the leading of the Lord. Refer to the Scriptures at the beginning of this section as you meditate on these truths. If you have questions about any of these concepts, turn to the Lord in prayer and ask Him for His understanding.

Satan perverts and distorts truth, usually in an incremental manner to disguise them, so I need to be on guard against those types of obscure distortions by asking for Your help and listening for Your truth continuously.

Satan offers me enticements and temptations as gifts that seem desirable to me in the moment of the offering, and they may be sweet to me initially, but they will soon turn bitter in my mouth.

Your love is the sweetest gift of all, and if I taste, I will see You are good.

Satan seeks to trick me into making covenant agreements with him, and attempts to hold me to these arrangements through accusation, legalism, and condemnation.

The enemy's tactics include deceiving me, then condemning me for believing and following the deception; stirring up fear or shame, ensnaring me in a prison that he describes as a hiding place of safety, then accusing me of building my own prison and choosing my own bondage; and, setting me up for failure by feeding my pride, convincing me I will be good enough or loved or accepted if I accomplish something in the world, then crushing my self-image when I fail.

Satan is a liar and a bully. You have empowered me to live in Your truth and to stand against the enemy. My strength is found in humility, the cross, and Your love for me.

Process

Process these suggested areas of focus based on this section. Remember, the goal is for you to grasp concepts, not develop a list of steps to take or rules to follow. If you understand the concepts, you will be able to see the whole picture, and can better understand any of its parts and apply the information presented to your own life. These suggestions may not match concepts that you valued from this section, so add your own concepts, based on beliefs and attitudes you have chosen to adopt from the reading and your time with the Lord, and applications that work for you. Incorporate these concepts in your daily meditations and prayer. As you synthesize and apply these concepts, combine them with the concepts you learned in the previous sections. Practice recalling each concept during times of adversity, and applying the concepts, with the Lord's help.

Synthesis: I choose to break any false agreements or covenant arrangements I have made with the enemy, through Your authority and by Your strength.

Application: When I feel bound to an enemy lie:

I will ask the Lord to reveal any covenants or agreements I have with the enemy.

I will ask for forgiveness for making the agreements, and through forgiveness I will prevent any enemy attempts to shame me for making the agreements.

I will break each agreement through prayer.

I will ask the Lord through prayer for truth to replace the broken agreements.

Synthesis: I choose to stand up in the face of Satan's bullying and lies by humbling myself, absorbing Your truth, and reveling in Your love.

Application: When I feel powerless under an enemy attack:

I will call out Satan's tactic for what it is.

I will remind myself that God is God and I am not.

I will speak out loud a relevant truth I already know to back the enemy off.

I will ask the Lord for new truth to use against the enemy's tactic.

I will rest in the Lord's love and receive His comfort as I recover from the attack.

Conclusion

In Section Four, we reviewed some typical enemy tactics and strategies. Satan plays on our vulnerabilities, seeking areas of weakness to gain access to our hearts. He then uses that access to promote increasingly damaging lies, often beginning with minor distortions of truth to disguise his attack until he has us whirling in confusion. Satan is basically a bully who has no real power, but who is using deception and manipulation to seek power through our agreement to give him our authority. We encourage you to stand up to the bully, recognizing he can do nothing to you as long as you refuse to believe him. As you walk through the Valley, humble yourself before God, not as a lesser creature unworthy of love, but as a beloved child who is given the status of co-heir with Christ. As you brave the Storm, melt into His truth like warm, soothing water, and fall into His loving arms. His love is the sweetest gift of all.

STRENGTH IN ADVERSITY

Now, let's learn about the armor God has given to us as protection against enemy onslaughts. As warriors fighting behind enemy lines, we need to be ready to use our weapons wisely, and to keep our defenses in place always. Practice using God's armor will help prepare us to stand.

STRENGTH IN ADVERSITY

FIVE

THE ARMOR OF GOD

Scripture

Remember to take time to read each verse carefully and in depth, not by rote, and to consider their application to facing adversity. Look up each verse, and read several verses leading up to and following the selection to understand the context. Ask what the Lord is wanting to say to you as you read these verses.

Ephesians 6:13-18 Therefore, put on the full armor of God, so that when the day of evil comes, you may be able to stand your ground, and after you have done everything, to stand. Stand firm then, with the belt of truth buckled around your waist, with the breastplate of righteousness in place, and with your feet fitted with the readiness that comes from the gospel of peace. In addition to all this, take up the shield of faith, with which you can extinguish all the flaming arrows of the evil one. Take the helmet of salvation and the sword of the Spirit, which is the word of God. And pray in the Spirit on all occasions with all kinds of prayers and requests.

I Corinthians 9:24-27 *Do you not know that in a race all the runners run, but only one gets the prize? Run in such a way as to get the prize. Everyone who competes in the games goes into strict training. They do it to get a crown that will not last, but we do it to get a crown that will last forever. Therefore, I do not run like someone running aimlessly; I do not fight like a boxer beating the air. No, I strike a blow to my body and make it my slave so that after I have preached to others, I myself will not be disqualified for the prize.*

Galatians 5:7 *You were running a good race. Who cut in on you to keep you from obeying the truth?*

I Thessalonians 5:16-18, 21-22 *Rejoice always, pray continually, give thanks in all circumstances; for this is God's will for you in Christ Jesus...hold on to what is good, reject every kind of evil.*

Romans 13:12 *The night is nearly over; the day is almost here. So let us put aside the deeds of darkness and put on the armor of light.*

I Thessalonians 5:5, 8 *You are all children of the light and children of the day. We do not belong to the night or to the darkness. But since we belong to the day, let us be sober, putting on faith and love as a breastplate, and the hope of salvation as a helmet.*

II Timothy 4:7 *I have fought the good fight, I have finished the race, I have kept the faith.*

Choose Your Weapons

We have discussed how the bombarding messages of the enemy and his worldly perspectives must be actively and intentionally fought. Any other position is acquiescence and we will lose ground to his deceptions. Satan is active and intentional in his war plans. He has agents surrounding us on every side. He knows details of our weaknesses, our vulnerabilities, and our easiest points of access. He strategizes for our downfall generations before we even exist. When we slumber our way through the war, or try to hide from its reality, we become easy targets, meat for his grinder. Nothing is hindering his extensive and purposeful plan, because that is our calling, and we are not showing up.

While God has provided us with effective weapons for the battle, we continue to respond to Satan's bomb-like strategies with the spiritual equivalent of a bow-and-arrow. How effective would it have been for someone on the front lines in World War II to stand in the open and fire arrows against the mortar, machine guns, and bombs of the opposing side? We don't seem to realize Jesus is our nuclear arsenal, and if we wield His weapons, the enemy doesn't stand a chance. But if we don't use the weapons provided, we are overcome by Satan's lies.

What would happen to soldiers if they were lackadaisical in their preparations, if they left their weapons behind or allowed them to collect dust, if they were lazy and undisciplined in their daily drill habits, if they failed to strategize for attacks against the enemy's positions and defense of their positions, if they did not listen for the directions of their leader, and if they did not trust their leader's directions? Yes, they would lose ground in the battle. And yes, we are losing ground.

We have become like Israel before their conquest by Babylon, as described by Jeremiah 6:10, 14-15: "To whom can I speak and give warning? Who will listen to me? Their ears are closed so they cannot hear. The word of the LORD is offensive to them; they find no pleasure in it. 'Peace, peace,' they say, when there is no peace. So they will fall among the fallen." What is the remedy? Jeremiah 6:16 states, "This is what the LORD says: 'Stand at the crossroads and look; ask for the ancient paths, ask where the good way is, and walk in it, and you will find rest for your souls.'" In this section, we will talk about "the good way;" in other words, fighting the good fight, what that looks like, what our weapons are, and how to use them effectively.

Paul outlined our armor and weapons for war in Ephesians 6:10-18. The weapons listed by Paul are truth, righteousness, peace, faith, salvation, the sword of the Spirit which is the word of God, and prayer. Let's use the example set by the apostles to walk in "the good way," by seeing how they utilized these weapons during their times of adversity.

The strength of the apostles. The apostles all fought the good fight, using the weapons Christ provided, with strength, fortitude, and passion. What were those weapons, and how can we use those same weapons to stand against the evil one? First, the apostles received the Holy Spirit; Jesus told them they would receive power when they received the One Who would lead them into all truth, and that only then would they become His witnesses (Acts 1:8). In other words, the presence of the Spirit of Christ in our hearts will empower us to stand, and without that presence, we will have no power and we will not be able to stand effectively.

Once the apostles received the Holy Spirit, they immediately began speaking truth and teaching others (Acts 2:32-33).

Truth. In a prior section, we discussed how truth is our best weapon against the three enemy lies of judgment, shame, and fear. We also discussed how every belief, every thought, and every feeling comes from and belongs to the realm of God, or comes from and belongs to the realm of the enemy; if we simply accept every thought, belief, or feeling as valid or true, or if we take ownership of every thought, belief, or feeling, we will lose the battle, because we will have already internalized whatever comes our way, and a good portion of what comes our way comes from the worldly perspective and the enemy's kingdom.

Paul described truth as our belt, meaning the part of our armor that secures and holds all our equipment in its proper place. As such, it is the most useful, versatile, important, and necessary aspect of our equipping by God to fight the enemy. The Holy Spirit is our primary source of truth. The Spirit speaks truth to our hearts, and brings Scripture alive for us, helping us to comprehend and interpret the teachings found there.

We can't trust our senses to give us truth, because they are of the worldly realm, and can be easily deceived. For example, hearing the words of others does not make those words true. Calling us short does not change our true heights of 6'(Donna) and 6'5" (David) tall. Others may say any words they want about us, but the only words we can count on are what we hear from Jesus.

Neither do experiences reveal truth, as they can be interpreted through a lie-based lens, and can be manipulated by the enemy to reinforce lies we believe. In the same way, we do not need to trust our own thoughts or feelings, because our thoughts can be easily deceived by the enemy, and our feelings, which arise from our beliefs, are only valid if they are the result of truth-based beliefs.

We need to examine every one of our beliefs, and weigh if it matches the truth we receive from the Holy Spirit. This type of awareness and examination takes discipline and intentionality, but mainly it requires a willingness to listen to the Holy Spirit over all other voices, including our own internal voice.

Finally, we need to always speak the truth. This may be harder than it sounds; however, if we speak lies, we invite the enemy, the father of lies, to come into our living room, and we are at that point in agreement with him and his realm. The consequences are our destruction. "Instead, speaking the truth in love, we will grow to become in every respect the mature body of him who is the head, that is, Christ" (Ephesians 4:15).

The truth is always stronger than the lie, purely because it is true. If we know the truth and it is deeply rooted in our hearts, anything that is lie-based will fail to pierce through it. As a result, we will be enabled to speak boldly and stand firm, because of our certainty and strength from His Spirit within us.

Righteousness. Our righteousness does not come from our own efforts to be good, because that would be a very poor breastplate indeed; instead, our righteousness is a result of the cross of Christ. In clothing ourselves with Christ (Galatians 3:27), we also are covered by His righteousness, and His righteousness becomes righteousness in us (Romans 3:22, II Corinthians 5:21). Through loving Christ, our hearts learn to love righteousness. It isn't about doing good; righteousness is the state of being in Christ.

Peace. The "gospel" or good news of peace is described by Paul as the truth of Christ's life, death, and resurrection to overcome death for us (I Corinthians 15:3-8). Once we no longer fear death because of death's defeat in Christ, we are free from fear and can truly live in peace. Accepting our freedom from death and living fully in that freedom, according to Paul, readies our feet to walk into battle.

In addition, the peace of God, a peace that transcends our understanding, is described by Paul as guarding our hearts and minds in Christ Jesus (Philippians 4:7). Now by peace, we do not mean the absence of conflict; instead, peace is the presence of an indescribable warmth and calm that flows through us from the Holy Spirit. We can employ His peace as a guard by first expecting to be at peace always. His peace cannot be swayed or overcome by adversity, but remains steadfast in our hearts, no matter what our circumstances. If we expect that kind of peace at all times, we will notice immediately anything that begins to push against it, even a little bit. We can then go to Jesus for help, protection, and truth to fully restore His peace. Like other weapons we have, monitoring our peace requires willingness and discipline on our part, but it is Christ in us Who empowers our peace.

Faith. In Hebrews 11:1, faith is defined for us as the certainty of things hoped for and the knowledge of things unseen. Being certain, therefore, of every truth we know from Jesus, and embracing those truths deep in our hearts, provides for us a shield that protects us in battle, preventing Satan's arrows, his well-aimed attempts to bring his lies into our hearts at our points of greatest vulnerability, from penetrating us and getting "in." Doubt is opposed to faith, and leaves holes in our shield. This is a sobering thought as we stand facing an enemy who has no compunction about attacking us at our weakest points. Before we get too discouraged, or let fear trip us up, let's consider Peter, who is well-known for having doubts.

When it came to interactions with Jesus, no one had more divergent and revealing responses than Peter. Peter was willing to get out of the boat and risk walking out onto water to get to Jesus, and immediately took his eyes off the Lord and sank, prompting Jesus to ask him, "why did you doubt?" (Matthew 14:31). Peter rightly identified Jesus as Messiah, which no one else either knew or was bold enough to claim, earning him the name "Rock" (Matthew 16:18), and promptly argued with Jesus that He wouldn't have to suffer and die, earning a strong rebuke from the Lord. Peter claimed he would follow Jesus anywhere, even into death, and promptly denied three times that he even knew Jesus (Luke 22:33-34). What a confusing mess of a man!

Peter was impulsive and audacious and inconsistent and outspoken and faltering and daring. Fear tripped him up again and again: on the waves, facing Jerusalem and potential suffering, at Gethsemane, and at Jesus' arrest. He doesn't sound like much of a rock. Even after the resurrection, he ran right back to his comfort zone. And once again, as if to say to Peter, "I know exactly who you are, my fisher of men, and I am reminding you who I told you I would make you by harkening back to our first day together," Jesus helped Peter to catch fish once again (John 21:4-6). Then Jesus redeemed Peter's denials by giving him three opportunities to express love for Jesus (John 21:15-17). Later, after Jesus ascended, the same Peter who, filled with the Holy Spirit, boldly returned to the steps of the Temple to preach after being imprisoned and warned never to preach again (Acts 5:18-21, 29), temporarily caved to peer pressure about once again following the Jewish Law (Galatians 2:11-21; Acts 15:1-2). You just never knew what you were going to get with Peter.

And so it is with us. We can take comfort from seeing that Jesus chose such an unpredictable jumble on which to build His church, and that He loved Peter, even with all his foibles and failures. So, when we doubt and become an unpredictable mess, we can think of Peter and remember that Jesus helped him to change the world. Even someone like Peter, when partnered with Jesus, can be amazing.

Salvation. In the same way peace readies our feet for battle, the knowledge of our salvation protects our thoughts and our minds, for if we are eternal children of God, what could Satan possibly do to us? "If God is for us, who can be against us? Who will bring any charge against those whom God has chosen? It is God who justifies. Who then is the one who condemns? No one. No, in all these things we are more than conquerors through him who loved us" (Romans 8:31, 33-34, 37). When the enemy tries to challenge our identity, or condemn us to entice us to return to judgment, we only need remember we are God's beloved children. We can return our thoughts to the fundamental truths that we are saved, we are redeemed, we are made new, and we are set free. These realities do not change, and there is nothing Satan can do about it.

The Word of God. Some people assume when the Word of God is mentioned in Scripture, it means the Bible; however, the Bible as we have it did not exist at the time Paul wrote this letter. Even in his description of this weapon, Paul makes it clear that the "sword" comes from the Holy Spirit, the One Who was sent to us to guide us into all truth (John 16:13). Thus, in this context, the weapon of warfare described here is the words and leading of the Holy Spirit in our hearts, providing what we need when we need it to be effective fighters. The sword of the Spirit is a weapon of offense, rather than protection or defense. This weapon is speaking the truth boldly to others, and openly waging war against the influence of the enemy in the world by expressing the light and truth of Christ, expressed in both word and deed.

Prayer. The final weapon mentioned is prayer. Prayer keeps us in communication and in relationship with Jesus. Without prayer, we are truly as warriors without a general; a leaderless flock of sheep wandering without our Shepherd, completely vulnerable to the wolf's attacks and led blindly to the slaughter. The need for prayer is so great, Paul instructs us to pray without ceasing (I Thessalonians 5:17). By prayer, however, he doesn't mean only asking and interceding; he is referring to listening to the directions of God during the battle.

Using our analogy of an army, how effective would the soldiers be if they sent requests to the leader, but the leader never replied, or if the soldiers were unaware of his reply? Communication with Jesus is two-way. It is relational, as He is relational by nature. In those ways, prayer is pivotal to our ability to fight the enemy and remain in God's truth.

These weapons are always ready and available for our use. If we find ourselves in our own Egypt, no matter what we have bound ourselves to, the Holy Spirit is more powerful, and His truth can walk us through the sea to freedom. If we walk through the fire of our own Babylon, we can know, no matter the circumstances or outcome, our righteousness in Christ insures our eternal safety and God's redemption. The Valley of illness is no threat to us, because the peace of God guards our hearts and minds from fear. In the midst of our Storm, we have faith, the certainty of things hoped for and the knowledge of things unseen, and in faith we can walk on water.

When enemies attack from all sides in our Berakah, we stand as children of God, and if God is for us, who can win against us? In our own Gethsemane of impending suffering, we can pull out our sword, and unlike Peter's sword, the sword of the Spirit will bring light and truth. And in our Wilderness, the place where we believe we are distant from God, or our Cave, where we have imprisoned ourselves to hide, or our Desert, where a sense of lack and feelings of being unloved overcome us, we can always reach out in prayer to our loving Father, Who will lead us out of the Wilderness, the Cave, or the Desert and into His loving arms.

Questions for Prayer

Now, we seek to prepare to use our weapons of war by asking the Lord for truth and listening for His responses to our questions. Our questions will explore the ideas presented in this section to insure their reliability, and will open us up to receive more truth that will continue to strengthen our stand. Remember, if you do not readily hear from the Lord, be patient with yourself and the process. Do not push to the point of frustration; extend yourself grace, take a break from listening when needed, move on from questions where you are getting stuck, and come back to those questions later.

Be sure to use your notebook to write down responses you receive from the Lord as you pray over each question. Don't trust your memory alone to retain every detail of what He shows you.

Lord, I ask that You would be with me as I seek to listen to Your voice and learn more about fighting the adversary with the weapons You have provided. Open my heart to receive Your truth, and guard my heart against the enemy's lies. Show me, Jesus...

1. In what ways have I been a lackadaisical soldier, not tending my weapons or listening to my leader?

2. Where is "the good way" for me in my life?

3. How does Your Spirit empower me to stand against the adversary?

4. In what ways does the belt of truth secure my other weapons?

5. What does it look like for You to be my righteousness?

6. How does Your peace guard my heart and mind?

7. In what ways am I like Peter, struggling between faith and doubt?

8. What does Your salvation of me tell me about my identity?

9. How do I take the offensive against the adversary?

10. How does prayer foster and develop my relationship with You?

Meditations

Spend time contemplating the ideas presented below, always keeping your heart and mind open to the leading of the Lord. Refer to the Scriptures at the beginning of this section as you meditate on these truths. If you have questions about any of these concepts, turn to the Lord in prayer and ask Him for His understanding.

The apostles demonstrated strength in standing against the evil one through reliance on Your presence in their hearts, and they waited on Your leading and followed Your direction on when, where, and what to teach.

The weapons You have provided are interdependent; they fuel each other, connect with each other, and interact with each other. For example, truth as one of our most powerful weapons has no power in our hearts without faith, because the truth loses any impact if we do not believe it.

I can use Your peace as a warning system to help me recognize when the enemy is attempting to bring a lie-based belief or thought. If I expect to be at peace, any disruption to that peace becomes my warning sign.

Your continued redemption of Peter's missteps demonstrates to me nothing is beyond Your salvation. I can trust in Your help every step of my way, and, like You loved Peter, I know You also love me and want to be my partner.

Your Spirit brings light and truth that cuts through any darkness or lie thrown my way by the enemy. I can wield Your sword defensively to fend off any attack, and proactively to further Your Kingdom. Continual prayer maintains my connection with Your Spirit.

Process

Process these suggested areas of focus based on this section. Remember, the goal is for you to grasp concepts, not develop a list of steps to take or rules to follow. If you understand the concepts, you will be able to see the whole picture, and can better understand any of its parts and apply the information presented to your own life. These suggestions may not match concepts that you valued from this section, so add your own concepts, based on beliefs and attitudes you have chosen to adopt from the reading and your time with the Lord, and applications that work for you. Incorporate these concepts in your daily meditations and prayer. As you synthesize and apply these concepts, combine them with the concepts you learned in the previous sections. Practice recalling each concept during times of adversity, and applying the concepts, with the Lord's help.

Synthesis: Recognizing the enemy is relentless, I choose to take care of the weapons You have given me for my defense against the enemy.

Application: Before I feel under enemy attack:

I will review and meditate on truths I have received from the Lord daily.

STRENGTH IN ADVERSITY

I will carefully consider my choices against the righteousness of Christ, and out of love for the Lord, I will choose righteousness to the best of my ability.

I will expect peace, and whenever peace wavers, I will immediately seek truth from the Lord.

I will exercise my faith and choose to believe the truth of the Lord over all other thoughts or voices.

I will contemplate the security of my salvation whenever I come under threat from circumstances, others, or the enemy.

I will listen to the Holy Spirit's whispers in my heart, and refuse to give weight to any other word.

Synthesis: I choose to pray continually.

Application: Each day from now on:

I will begin my day by greeting the Lord and asking for His input on the course of my day.

I will take time to listen as I move through each part of my day.

I will ask the Lord about all challenges that may arise.

I will seek truth from the Lord at the first sign of my peace being disturbed.

Conclusion

In Section Five, we studied the full armor of God. We recognize how Satan relentlessly attacks our vulnerabilities, seeking areas of weakness to gain access to our hearts. Knowing this, we see how important it is to practice using the weapons God has provided for us, and to keep those weapons in a state of readiness for use. The weapons we use are truth, righteousness, peace, faith, salvation, the Holy Spirit, and prayer. These weapons are interdependent; none of them stand alone. In the same way, we do not take our stand against the enemy alone; instead, we rely on God and depend on His help and presence to guard our hearts and minds. We encourage you to exercise as you would if you were working out, training for a competition. As you walk through the Valley, pray without ceasing, remember His truth, and allow His peace to be your guard. As you brave the Storm, keep your eyes on Him, and do not give weight to any other voice, believing His word alone. Above all else, every morning, every evening, and all through your day, remember that you are loved by God.

Now, let's learn about the underpinnings of all our weapons, and why these weapons work. Spoiler alert: it may not be what you think!

SIX

CHOICE & FREEDOM

Scripture

Remember to take time to read each verse carefully and in depth, not by rote, and to consider their application to facing adversity. Look up each verse, and read several verses leading up to and following the selection to understand the context. Ask what the Lord is wanting to say to you as you read these verses.

Deuteronomy 30:19-20 *This day I call the heavens and the earth as witnesses against you that I have set before you life and death, blessings and curses. Now choose life, so that you and your children may live and that you may love the LORD your God, listen to his voice, and hold fast to him. For the LORD is your life.*

Proverbs 8:10-11 *Choose my instruction instead of silver, knowledge rather than choice gold, for wisdom is more precious than rubies, and nothing you desire can compare with her.*

Romans 8:5-6 *Those who live according to the flesh have their minds set on what the flesh desires; but those who live in accordance with the Spirit have their minds set on what the Spirit* *desires. The mind governed by the flesh is death, but the mind governed by the Spirit is life and peace.*

James 4:4 *Don't you know that friendship with the world means enmity against God? Therefore, anyone who chooses to be a friend of the world becomes an enemy of God.*

I Corinthians 10:23-24, 31 *"I have the right to do anything," you say—but not everything is beneficial. "I have the right to do anything"—but not everything is constructive. No one should seek their own good, but the good of others. Whatever you do, do it all for the glory of God.*

Galatians 5:13-14, 16-17 *You, my brothers and sisters, were called to be free. But do not use your freedom to indulge the flesh; rather, serve one another humbly in love. For the entire law is fulfilled in keeping this one command: "Love your neighbor as yourself." So I say, walk by the Spirit, and you will not gratify the desires of the flesh. For the flesh desires what is contrary to the Spirit, and the Spirit what is contrary to the flesh.*

II Corinthians 3:17-18 *Now the Lord is the Spirit, and where the Spirit of the Lord is, there is freedom. And we all, who with unveiled faces contemplate the Lord's glory, are being transformed into his image with ever-increasing glory, which comes from the Lord, who is the Spirit.*

Choose Your Life

Choice is the underpinning of all warfare. Choice is the foundation of all our weaponry. The basis of our ability to wage war against the enemy of God is our free will. Our ability to choose is what enables us to be able to fight at all. Choice makes it impossible for the enemy to control us, to "make" us do anything, or to determine outcomes in our lives. Because we are able to choose, we can always choose God, and we can always choose to refuse the enemy and his tactics.

So, let's go back to the beginning, where God gave us that free will choice. First, we need to understand the importance of choice and how it impacts our relationship with God. Knowing that we could, and indeed would, choose to accept the original lie of the enemy that we could be like God, why would God give us that choice? The answer is found in the alternative. If we did not have the freedom to choose, we would be unable to love, because of how love is defined. Love requires the ability to choose to freely give it. If we cannot freely give it, it is not love. Love cannot be mandated. Love cannot be controlled or forced, and still be love.

The root of our free will is God's love for us, and because God is in His very nature love, He would do nothing else but give us the freedom to choose to love Him – or not – which means we have the very real choice to sin against God and to believe we can be god of our own lives. We continue to have that very same choice to this day.

It is the wisdom and redeeming nature and power of God that He uses what brought us destruction and death as the ultimate defeat of death; the very thing that gave us the ability to choose to sin against Him is the thing that gives us the ability to choose Him, to love Him, and to reject the enemy.

Jesus makes us partners with God, active participants in the war against evil, and if we choose against Satan and his forces and his lies, guess what? There is not one thing Satan can do about it! Free will gives us the ability to fight the enemy and removes all his power in our lives. Jesus demonstrated this truth for us by His free will choice in the garden of Gethsemane to take the cup of suffering, to walk the path to Calvary, and to die on the cross to remove our shame, which undid the results of our original sin, and by His resurrection, which defeated death, the consequence of that sin.

As it states in Hebrews 2:14-15, "Since the children have flesh and blood, he too shared in their humanity so that by his death he might break the power of him who holds the power of death— that is, the devil— and free those who all their lives were held in slavery by their fear of death." Further, in Romans 8:15-17, Paul writes, "The Spirit you received does not make you slaves, so that you live in fear again; rather, the Spirit you received brought about your adoption to sonship. And by him we cry, *'Abba,* Father.' The Spirit himself testifies with our spirit that we are God's children. Now if we are children, then we are heirs—heirs of God and co-heirs with Christ, if indeed we share in his sufferings in order that we may also share in his glory." And in Philippians 3:10, Paul proclaims, "I want to know Christ—yes, to know the power of his resurrection and participation in his sufferings, becoming like him in his death."

Satan knows the power of our choice, and as a result is constantly trying to convince us that our choices are limited, or powerless, or fruitless. The usurper of Christ's authority also attempts to usurp our Christ-given authority, trying to convince us to feel it doesn't matter what we choose, and as a result, to feel like we don't matter; and, trying to get us to believe we don't have a choice. But herein is the beauty of God's redemption: Satan can't "make" us feel or believe anything, because we always have a choice!

Instead of the should's, ought to's, have to's, and can'ts of judgment, fear, and shame, God has given us "want to" and "choose to" as replacements. These phrases are the expressions of freedom in our language. We are free to be fully and completely who God made us to be, and we are free to choose according to our true hearts – not according to our "flesh" or sin nature, but out of the overflow of Christ living within our hearts. We are free from restriction to our choices based on shame and condemnation, or based on external expectations or demands.

Some may say, like those who opposed Paul, that God still expects us to uphold His law, or that God still requires us to follow the Law to be saved, rather than declaring with our mouths that Jesus is Lord and believing in our hearts that God raised Him from the dead to be saved (Romans 10:9-10). However, that belief does not agree with Scripture. "Therefore, there is now no condemnation for those who are in Christ Jesus, because through Christ Jesus the law of the Spirit who gives life has set you free from the law of sin and death" (Romans 8:1-2).

Those who still focus on the law are bound to fear. They fear judgment, and they fear true freedom will result in chaos or licentiousness. Paul received the same arguments: "What shall we say, then? Shall we go on sinning so that grace may increase? By no means! We are those who have died to sin; how can we live in it any longer? What then? Shall we sin because we are not under the law but under grace? By no means! Don't you know that when you offer yourselves to someone as obedient slaves, you are slaves of the one you obey—whether you are slaves to sin, which leads to death, or to obedience, which leads to righteousness? But thanks be to God that, though you used to be slaves to sin, you have come to obey from your heart the pattern of teaching that has now claimed your allegiance. You have been set free from sin and have become slaves to righteousness" (Romans 6:1-2, 15-18). Paul's response highlights how we are free from the law, and we are also free from slavery to sin, because we follow Christ in our hearts.

We are truly free from the law because the law has been fulfilled in Christ. As Jesus said, "Do not think that I have come to abolish the Law or the Prophets; I have not come to abolish them but to fulfill them" (Matthew 5:17), and as Paul said, "For all who rely on the works of the law are under a curse… Christ redeemed us from the curse of the law by becoming a curse for us" (Galatians 3:10, 13). If we follow God's law, it is because we truly know His instructions are for our good, for our protection, for our benefit, and for our well-being, not because we fear God's judgment or feel forced into it. We are led by the Spirit, and desire what the Spirit desires (Romans 8:5, Galatians 5:17).

In that way, our heart's desires inform our choices, and the law is rendered irrelevant. For example, if we have no desire to commit murder, we do not need a law telling us not to murder. We are free, then, to follow our true hearts' desires. We choose to love God with all our hearts because our hearts do love Him; we choose to love ourselves because we know how much He loves us; we choose to love our neighbors as ourselves because His love has permeated our hearts and overflows into others. Actions motivated by fear are limited to the presence of some punishment, an external source of control. Choices motivated by love are truly free.

The same love that gave us the wonderful gifts of choice and freedom also provided the equally wonderful gifts of responsibility and accountability. In fact, without responsibility there can be no freedom. The truth of God says we are responsible for our own choices. "Do not be deceived: God cannot be mocked. A man reaps what he sows" (Galatians 6:7). God built responsibility into the fabric of creation, even expressed as a law of physics, that actions produce reactions.

The reason God created such a system was out of love for us. Imagine for a moment what our lives would be like if our actions produced no predictable results. How could we ever learn what is beneficial and what is harmful? Without the resulting consequences from our choices, we would be repeating the same harmful actions, but never learning. We would also be living in a world ruled by chaos, without order and without understanding or wisdom.

So, it was love that determined choice and consequence, which gave us responsibility, and in so doing produced real freedom. Accountability, then, is part of love, and removing responsibility or consequences for choices ultimately removes freedom.

Responsibility, however, is not the same thing as fault or blame. Fault and blame are aspects of the lie of shame, which is from the enemy. Fault says, "I am bad;" responsibility says, "yes, that was a poor choice I made." Thus, responsibility gives us the freedom to make a different choice next time, or to make amends for our poor choices. Fault, by contrast, traps us in the bad choice like quicksand, and we keep repeating the same poor decisions.

Not taking responsibility may look attractive on the surface, especially if we equate responsibility with shame. After all, taking responsibility seems hard, and we like to avoid difficulty. We don't want to feel bad. Instead, we prefer to defend ourselves, or to point to others to take the fall. However, the satisfaction or relief is short-lived, because consequences start happening anyway, even if we don't choose to accept responsibility for our choices. Shame binds us to repeating the same behavior, and self-justification or blame keeps us from seeing what we need to change and realizing that we can change. In these ways, our choices are restricted and our freedom is lost.

True freedom does not come from avoidance of responsibility; it comes from accepting responsibility, and receiving all the very valuable lessons that grow us in that process. Choice, freedom, responsibility, and accountability are all integrally connected. Losing any of these valuable gifts means losing all of them, binding us once more as slaves to sin. But we know, "It is for freedom that Christ has set us free. Stand firm, then, and do not let yourselves be burdened again by a yoke of slavery" (Galatians 5:1).

To stand strong in the face of adversity, and continue to live in freedom, we must live in accordance with the Spirit. But what does it mean to live in accordance with the Spirit? Paul tells us that "those who live in accordance with the Spirit have their minds set on what the Spirit desires" (Romans 8:5). To truly have our minds set on what His Spirit desires, we need to be in continuous connection and communication with Him, at all times, and about all things.

We cannot continue to rely on our own perceptions, interpretations, opinions, viewpoints, past experiences, or present circumstances to inform our minds. We want to see through the Spirit's eyes, interpret only through His truth, and formulate our views and opinions based on what we hear Him saying and what we know He has said. We no longer want to give weight to this physical "reality" that our senses perceive, giving all the weight to the spiritual reality that our spirits perceive through the presence of His Spirit in us, such that our circumstances no longer have power over our feelings. Instead, it is His presence, His love for us, and His peace that influences our feelings.

As Paul explains in Romans 8:10, "But if Christ is in you, then even though your body is subject to death because of sin, the Spirit gives life because of righteousness." Even the death of our bodies has no power in our lives. In the same way, all aspects of the "flesh" lose power as we live in accordance with the Spirit.

To live by the Spirit, we need to be relationship-focused and process-focused. To be relationship-focused is to make our choices based on the question, "What is the loving thing to do?" As Paul states in I Corinthians 16:14, "Do everything in love." Because we are God's children and heirs, we are given the inheritance of His love in our hearts, which if we allow, flows freely to others. According to Romans 8:16, "The Spirit himself testifies with our spirit that we are God's children." What a beautiful foundation from which to live! God is a relational God, and His focus is on His relationship with us and our relationships with each other. If we live by the Spirit, His focus becomes our focus.

To live focused on processes means to live attentive to the deeper things, the things underlying the surface actions or behaviors, such as motivations, values, purpose, and foundational beliefs. Processes are like the roots of the tree, and all other, superficial things are the leaves and branches. When we focus on the surface things, like behaviors, words, results, circumstances, and outcomes, we become like gardeners who prune branches and trim leaves, but the tree continues to grow back year after year, because the root is still intact, so nothing really changes.

Process-focus allows us to go deeper, under the surface, where our "fruit" is determined. In the deeper places in our hearts, Jesus, if invited, can make transformational changes, so our root values and beliefs match His own, and our motivations and purposes in life are growing out of truth.

Paul explains this deep-level change in Romans 8:7-9 in this way: "The mind governed by the flesh is hostile to God; it does not submit to God's law, nor can it do so. Those who are in the realm of the flesh cannot please God. You, however, are not in the realm of the flesh but are in the realm of the Spirit, if indeed the Spirit of God lives in you." Paul goes on, in Romans 12:2, to instruct us, "Do not conform to the pattern of this world, but be transformed by the renewing of your mind. Then you will be able to test and approve what God's will is—his good, pleasing and perfect will."

Finally, to truly live in accordance with the Spirit, we must recognize our need. Our inabilities, separate from God, in all things, and the presence of original sin engraved in our flesh or sin nature must be acknowledged, from a place of humility and brokenness. We are asked to "put to death the misdeeds of the body" by the Spirit (Romans 8:13). The foundational "misdeed" of our flesh is our desire to be our own god of our lives, just as Adam and Eve sought to "be like God, knowing good and evil" in the garden. From this sin of the flesh, all other sins arise. It is the "process-level" sin in all of us, the root of all our sin behaviors, and it must be crucified in us. As Paul described, "I have been crucified with Christ and I no longer live, but Christ lives in me" (Galatians 2:20).

Only when we accept that we are not God can we truly live by the Spirit. We must exchange our desire to be our own god for reliance on Christ. To some, that might seem like a loss, like giving up something important, or sacrificing our personhood; however, the paradox of the Kingdom of God is that in order to gain our lives, we must lose our lives, and if we lose our lives for His sake we will find life. It is in this place where our desire to be God dies that we can find who we really are, and where we can finally and truly be free.

Now we have come full circle in our discussion on the adversity of warfare. With the underpinning of our God-ordained and God-given free will choice, we have the ground on which to stand against the enemy and all his schemes. If we choose to love God and seek His truth as our best weapon, and if we choose to live according to His truth, Satan's plans crumble. Satan may be a master manipulator and a skilled liar, but as it is with any magic trick, once you know how it is done, and you can see through the smoke and mirrors, the trick loses its power and its interest. None of Satan's lies or manipulations or deceptions or schemes can stand when the light of truth reveals their reality. The weapons of war, provided by the Holy Spirit, are effective simply because we can choose to wield them.

So, whether we are slaves in our own Egypt, walking through fire in our own Babylon, weeping in our own Gethsemane, or suffering at our own Calvary, we can choose how we respond. No Wilderness can keep us from the presence of Christ. No Valley can consume us in shadow. No Cave can separate us from God's love. No Storm can engulf us. No Tomb can hold us. "No, in all these things we are more than conquerors through him who loved us. For I am convinced that neither death nor life, neither angels nor demons, neither the present nor the future, nor any powers, neither height nor depth, nor anything else in all creation, will be able to separate us from the love of God that is in Christ Jesus our Lord" (Romans 8:37-39).

What will you choose?

Questions for Prayer

Now, we seek to prepare to live in freedom by asking the Lord for truth and listening for His responses to our questions. Our questions will explore the ideas presented in this section to insure their reliability, and will open us up to receive more truth that will continue to strengthen our stand. Remember, if you do not readily hear from the Lord, be patient with yourself and the process. Do not push to the point of frustration; extend yourself grace, take a break from listening when needed, move on from questions where you are getting stuck, and come back to those questions later.

Be sure to use your notebook to write down responses you receive from the Lord as you pray over each question. Don't trust your memory alone to retain every detail of what He shows you.

Lord, I ask that You would be with me as I seek to listen to Your voice and learn more about exercising my freedom to choose. Open my heart to receive Your truth, and guard my heart against the enemy's lies. Show me, Jesus...

1. In what ways does my ability to choose impact my ability to fight against the adversary?

2. What is the connection between choice and love?

3. How are my daily choices like the choice made by Adam and Eve?

4. What are some ways the enemy has usurped the authority You gave to me?

5. How is taking responsibility for my choices related to freedom?

6. What does Paul mean when he instructs me to have my mind set on what You desire?

7. What does it look like to live a relationship-focused life?

8. What are some of the deeper processes You would want me to remain focused on?

9. What does brokenness mean in the context of recognizing my need for You?

10. How do I "lose" my life?

Meditations

Spend time contemplating the ideas presented below, always keeping your heart and mind open to the leading of the Lord. Refer to the Scriptures at the beginning of this section as you meditate on these truths. If you have questions about any of these concepts, turn to the Lord in prayer and ask Him for His understanding.

My freedom to choose is vital to my victory over the enemy; You made it impossible for the enemy to control me because I always have a choice.

You have set me free from slavery to the law. Nothing is required or mandated beyond knowing You as Lord, and a heart-level belief in Your resurrection. I am free to choose based solely on loving You, and allowing Your love to flow from my heart.

Because You live within me, I can live by Your Spirit, relationship-focused and process-focused in my life, and my heart is transformed at its root. I can be free from fear, shame, and condemnation and all the beliefs that go with them.

Responsibility goes along with choice and freedom. I am responsible for my choices, and for the consequences that follow. Taking responsibility rather than self-justifying or blaming others prevents the enemy from gaining a foothold, which limits my freedom.

When I live in accordance with Your Spirit, my heart's desires can inform my choices, and my choices are motivated by love. Living by Your Spirit is living in true freedom.

Process

Process these suggested areas of focus based on this section. Remember, the goal is for you to grasp concepts, not develop a list of steps to take or rules to follow. If you understand the concepts, you will be able to see the whole picture, and can better understand any of its parts and apply the information presented to your own life. These suggestions may not match concepts that you valued from this section, so add your own concepts, based on beliefs and attitudes you have chosen to adopt from the reading and your time with the Lord, and applications that work for you. Incorporate these concepts in your daily meditations and prayer. As you synthesize and apply these concepts, combine them with the concepts you learned in the previous sections. Practice recalling each concept during times of adversity, and applying the concepts, with the Lord's help.

Synthesis: I choose to fiercely and diligently protect my freedom, to prevent the adversary from usurping my God-given authority.

Application: When faced with a choice:

I will intentionally exercise my God-ordained right to choose, instead of passively waiting for life to happen to me.

I will use the language of choice in my daily vocabulary, such as "I choose," "I want," and "I desire."

I will make a list of multiple options, even outlandish ones, to remind myself I do have a choice.

I will consider the consequences of my choices prior to choosing.

I will take responsibility for my choices and accept the consequences of my choices.

I will reject any shame or condemnation from the enemy based on my choices, knowing I am free to choose differently and to make amends.

Synthesis: I choose to live in accord with Your Spirit, maintaining my focus on relationship with You and others, and on processes, such as values, motivations, and my true heart's desires.

Application: Each day from now on:

I will rely on the Lord's Spirit within me to guide my steps by relinquishing my attempts to control and self-determine.

I will admit my need for the Lord, and approach the Lord from a position of brokenness.

I will ask to see everything through the Lord's eyes, and watch and listen for His vision and understanding to come to me.

I will follow the desires of my true heart and reject the desires of the flesh when they seek to influence my choices.

Conclusion

In Section Six, we examined the central underpinning in our stand against adversity: choice. Our freedom to choose is God-ordained and God-given, and without it, the enemy could plunder us without restriction or limit. However, because of God's gift of free will, we are free to say no to the enemy, no matter what stunt he pulls. We are also free to love, to choose Christ, and to live from our true hearts. Choice, responsibility, and freedom are integrally connected, each one requiring the other two to be fully realized. We encourage you to continuously exercise your freedom to choose, reminding yourself often that you always have a choice, and using the language of choice in your speaking and thinking. As you walk through the Valley, choose to focus on love as the motivation for your responses. As you brave the Storm, choose to walk in agreement with the Spirit instead of reacting based on the flesh. His freedom is the most precious gift of all.

Now that we walk in freedom, let's learn how to frame our thoughts in a way that results in joy and peace. As allies to freedom, joy and peace will help us to continue to stand.

SEVEN

JOY & PEACE

Scripture

Remember to take time to read each verse carefully and in depth, not by rote, and to consider their application to facing adversity. Look up each verse, and read several verses leading up to and following the selection to understand the context. Ask what the Lord is wanting to say to you as you read these verses.

Galatians 5:22-25 But the fruit of the Spirit is love, joy, peace, forbearance, kindness, goodness, faithfulness, gentleness and self-control. Against such things there is no law. Those who belong to Christ Jesus have crucified the flesh with its passions and desires. Since we live by the Spirit, let us keep in step with the Spirit.

Nehemiah 8:10 ...for the joy of the LORD is your strength.

Psalm 95:1-2 Come, let us sing for joy to the LORD; let us shout aloud to the Rock of our salvation. Let us come before him with thanksgiving and extol him with music and song.

Philippians 4:12-13 *I know what it is to be in need, and I know what it is to have plenty. I have learned the secret of being content in any and every situation, whether well fed or hungry, whether living in plenty or in want. I can do all this through him who gives me strength.*

Colossians 3:12-15 *Therefore, as God's chosen people, holy and dearly loved, clothe yourselves with compassion, kindness, humility, gentleness and patience. Bear with each other and forgive one another if any of you has a grievance against someone. Forgive as the Lord forgave you. And over all these virtues put on love, which binds them all together in perfect unity. Let the peace of Christ rule in your hearts, since as members of one body you were called to peace. And be thankful.*

Matthew 6:27, 34 *Can any one of you by worrying add a single hour to your life? Therefore, do not worry about tomorrow, for tomorrow will worry about itself. Each day has enough trouble of its own.*

The Joy of the Lord

Our perception of a work of art is altered by the frame we put around it, and by the perspective from which we view it. If we choose a cheap, plain, black metal frame for our picture, and use a plain white piece of paper to serve as a border, the whole painting seems cheapened, and we perceive it as mundane and common. If we stand two inches from the picture, such that all we can see is the bottom left corner, we will completely miss the whole, and to us, the painting will appear to be a meaningless blotch of one color. However, even a common print begins to look beautiful when displayed with expensive mats and an ornate frame. When we stand back and look at the whole picture, we can experience its true beauty, and comprehend the artist's perspective.

In the same way, the frame we place around our thoughts, and the perspective we use to view our circumstances alters our perceptions. Our frame of mind matters, and our perspective and point of view impacts what we see, and how we feel.

Scripture has a lot to say about how we "clothe" our mind and what perspectives to bring to bear on our experiences. In this section, we will explore specifically the framework and perspectives that produce joy and peace. We suggest adopting these Scriptural positions through "taking every thought captive to make it obedient to Christ" (II Corinthians 10:5) because how we choose to focus our thoughts directly produces how we feel.

Gratitude. Thankfulness and gratitude involves not focusing on things you don't have, things that go wrong, or circumstances you didn't expect, but instead focusing on things you do have, things that go right, and how circumstances are being redeemed. Our circumstances do not get to determine who we are, how we feel, or what we choose. Because God has ordained that we have the freedom to choose, we have both the right and the responsibility to walk our own path based on who God created us to be, rather than basing our choices on what others think of us, what others do, or what happens to us in our circumstances.

Scripture would not suggest we give thanks in all circumstances unless it was possible for us to do so. In difficulty, we can choose to focus on those things outside of us that are happening to us, or we can choose to focus our hearts and minds on what Jesus has done for us, His love for us, His presence with us in the midst of the circumstances, and every good thing He has provided for us, because these things are unchanging and ever-present in our lives.

Gratitude is not possible, however, without our acknowledgement that we need help. The truth is, we need Another. We are built for relationship. If we believe it is all up to us and we are in it alone, or if we believe we can save ourselves or do enough to "earn" love, or determine our own value and worth, or protect ourselves, we will miss the great gifts of Jesus' love, His protection, and His valuing of us. We won't perceive these things, because our eyes will be focused on ourselves.

Instead, we will foster resentment in our hearts, because these beliefs leave us feeling like we "should" do it ourselves or we "have to" do it on our own, and we will feel fear and shame instead of feeling loved and loving. Resentment is the antithesis of gratitude.

So, we encourage you to choose to focus your hearts on those things that are stable and sure, such as who God is and who He says you are, and on those things that are good and right and true. Then, express your gratitude for those many gifts. Once you have fixed your eyes on God's great gifts, check your feelings, and see if you don't begin to feel peace and joy. "Finally, brothers and sisters, whatever is true, whatever is noble, whatever is right, whatever is pure, whatever is lovely, whatever is admirable—if anything is excellent or praiseworthy—think about such things" (Philippians 4:8).

Perseverance. It is interesting to note that joyous and peaceful people are rarely those who have experienced little or no difficulty; they are not the ones who have had it "easy." Paradoxically, people whose lives have been relatively easy or without struggle often are quite dissatisfied, feel quickly overwhelmed, tend to give up readily, and feel entitled to things continuing to be easy. These people often do not know how to cope or respond when difficulties arise, and consistently seek the easy road instead of the righteous or truth-based road. But difficulty will arise for all eventually.

Rather than avoiding or ignoring difficulties, joyous and peaceful people are those who persevere in the face of struggles, and walk through struggles to the end with Jesus. Through perseverance, we begin to see we can live beyond our perceived limits, and our view of ourselves is altered.

One of the "roles" the enemy suggests we play is the Victim role. Several elements make up this role, including abdicating responsibility, giving up freedom to choose, powerlessness, blame of others or circumstances, hopelessness, helplessness, and paralysis. Perseverance demonstrates to us we are not victims, we can push ourselves farther than we first believed, we are capable of more than we realize, and we are worth fighting for. According to Paul, perseverance produces character in us; in other words, inner strength, and the ability to stand up, take responsibility, and face adversity with honor, discipline, and values.

In the face of perseverance, circumstances lose their "power." We begin to see ourselves as Victors instead of Victims. At the same time, our view of God changes, as we realize it is by His strength we have overcome.

We have a choice, then. Will we agree with the enemy to be the Victim of life, where circumstances dictate how we feel and what we do, and lie down, give up, and give in; or, will we partner with Jesus, stand up in the face of suffering with Him by our side, and persevere through the struggle to the other side? Will we fix our eyes on the circumstances, or on Jesus? We encourage you to persevere, so that you may learn that you have the strength of the presence of Christ within you to rely on. Joy and peace are the results. "Consider it pure joy, my brothers and sisters, whenever you face trials of many kinds, because you know that the testing of your faith produces perseverance" (James 1:2-3).

Contentment. Some may think that an attitude of contentment arises from things going how we want them to go, having everything we want, feeling "as good as" someone else, or an absence of difficulties; however, this is not the case. Contentment, like every other frame of reference, is a choice.

If we rely on external things, such as the approval of others or circumstances working out just how we want, to determine our feelings, then we abdicate our personal choice and give away all our authority to those external sources, whether those are people, circumstances, or the enemy. Do you see how transient and temporary our joy and peace would be? Any little thing could come along and disrupt our peace, and the worldly state, based in sin, gains great power over our lives. Yet, Jesus came to alleviate the impact of sin, so clearly basing contentment on external sources is not what He had in mind.

Comparing ourselves to others is destructive to joy and peace. We can't find contentment through achieving a positive comparison to someone else, whether we are comparing their abilities to ours, or their achievements, or their circumstances and outcomes. Jealousy and dissatisfaction lead to discontentment. In contrast, knowing who God made you to be, and choosing to be who He created you to be in every situation, leads to peace and joy.

God made each of us by His hand, with intentionality and purpose, and with a distinctive, specific set of thoughts and desires in mind for us. He absolutely adores who He made us to be; therefore, it is a joyful thing to experience and share God's feelings about ourselves, "for we are God's handiwork" (Ephesians 2:10).

Galatians 6:4 says, "Each one should test their own actions. Then they can take pride in themselves alone, without comparing themselves to someone else." Other versions translate the word rendered pride as "rejoicing" in themselves alone. What Paul meant by "taking pride in (our)selves alone" is finding joy and contentment in being who we are in Christ. Being content with who He made while knowing we are each a one-of-a-kind work of art is a peace-generating outlook.

We are also called to achieve contentment separate from our circumstances. Paul draws the conclusion in Philippians 4:12-13 that contentment means a focus on Christ, and a reliance on His strength, no matter what our circumstances may be. Paul is clear that contentment isn't having plenty; in fact, having plenty and being in need are presented side-by-side as if they are one in the same. Our circumstances are a setting in which we have our relationship with Jesus, like the set for a play. The play doesn't revolve around the set; the play simply takes place on the set.

Our relationship with Christ is unchanging, not swayed by circumstantial variations, which gives us a solid and secure foundation on which to stand, no matter what happens in our lives. Knowing where our feet are anchored, and feeling the resulting sense of safety and certainty, gives us a strong and assured peace. It isn't the absence of difficulty that gives this peace. It is living one with Christ.

An attitude of contentment, then, is about knowing who we are according to Christ, focusing on and living based on who we are in all situations, and relying on the consistency of love in the presence of Christ for our strength, our assurance, and our stability. "Godliness with contentment is great gain" (I Timothy 6:6).

Acceptance. From walking through experiences of grief to seeing others as Jesus sees them to receiving truth from the Holy Spirit in our hearts, acceptance produces deep peace and lasting joy. By acceptance, we are not referring to passivity. Ask, seek, and knock are actions verbs; indeed, Jesus demonstrated an active and intentional journey during His life, His face always turned toward His purpose and goal. Passivity is more like acquiescence and resignation than acceptance.

The well-known Serenity Prayer says it well: "God grant me the serenity to accept the things I cannot change; courage to change the things I can; and wisdom to know the difference." The prayer continues: "Living one day at a time; enjoying one moment at a time; accepting hardships as the pathway to peace; taking, as He did, this sinful world as it is, not as I would have it; trusting that He will make all things right if I surrender to His Will; that I may be reasonably happy in this life and supremely happy with Him forever in the next. Amen."[3] Niebuhr is describing acceptance as he saw mirrored in the life of Christ.

Seeing things as they are and accepting things we cannot change, such as the death of a loved one, or any other circumstance beyond our control or influence, is, as Niebuhr indicated, the pathway to peace. Railing against the wind and trying to stop the tides are futile and frustrating endeavors. Instead, we can choose to experience the wind and tide as lovely parts of life, changing our perspective which also changes our response.

Acceptance also refers to the way we receive truth we hear from the Holy Spirit. Jesus described different ways of receiving truth in His parable of the sower (Mark 4:2-9, 14-20). In our hearts, we can choose if His truth falls on the path where Satan will snatch it away, among the rocks where the seed doesn't take root and withers under trial, among the thorns and weeds where worry and worldliness choke it out, or in the good soil where we "hear the word, accept it, and produce a crop – a hundred times what was sown" (Mark 4:20).

Finally, acceptance means seeing others through Christ's eyes, and receiving them as He receives them. To do this form of acceptance requires asking Jesus to reveal to us, for each person we meet, who He created them to be. We are specifically instructed not to judge others (Matthew 7:1-5). Satan, however, wants us to take on the role of Judge. As Jesus indicates in this teaching, it is important to note that when we judge ourselves, we will also judge others. Judgment flowing into us means judgment flowing out of us, and vice versa. Instead, as we live fully from our hearts, being who God created us to be, in the same way we want to accept fully in our hearts who God created others to be. "Accept one another, then, just as Christ accepted you, in order to bring praise to God (Romans 15:7).

Surrender. Surrender is about letting go of the illusion of control. As long as we believe that we have control over anything, we will create anxiety within us which destroys our peace and robs our joy. We need to accept there is no such thing as control. We like to hedge around this issue with such statements as "I don't control others, but I am in control of myself" or "I'm not in control but God is in control." In buying into these thoughts, we are continuing the illusion that there is such a thing as control. There is not.

God is Sovereign, which means He has the authority and right to rule, but He does not determine outcomes, because He has given us free will along with a role as participants in the working out of His will.[4] Satan also exerts his usurped authority to impact things in this world, if he can get us to cooperate by believing his lies. Thus, many factors impact what happens and how things turn out. We have no control because control does not exist. Our action does not determine an outcome, and God's will is not always done on earth as it is in heaven, which is why Jesus instructed us to pray for God's will to be done.

What do we have, then, if there is no such thing as control? What are we surrendering to? God asks us to surrender our whole selves into His hands and His heart. He asks that we walk with Him through every circumstance, no matter what the outcome, knowing and trusting that He loves us. Trying to control and worrying about outcomes; in other words, approaching life with fear; destroys peace.

God gives us choice to replace control, so making choices without an expectation of a particular outcome, and resting with God after making the best possible choices we can make according to His guidance and leadership, increases our joy and peace. We have a partner Who loves us dearly as His precious children. Rather than trying to control, which ultimately fails, doesn't it make more sense to abide with Him, listen to His voice in every circumstance, and walk through every situation holding His strong hand? When we choose this path, outcomes are not as important as the journey itself, and being with Him is everything. "Cast all your anxiety on Him because he cares for you" (1 Peter 5:7).

Forgiveness. Forgiveness is often misunderstood as meaning the sin against you doesn't matter or didn't happen, or the sinner is let "off the hook" for the sin. Jesus is clear that He hates sin, and desires that no one would sin. Sin matters in that sin has real consequences in our lives and in the lives of those around us.

Instead, forgiveness simply means we know we are not the judge; instead, we allow Jesus to take the sin committed against us so we don't have to carry it, and we know and trust He will deal with it well because He is a just God. We need to always remember we have been forgiven much, so we also want to forgive others. At times, when someone sins against us and we suffer the consequences of the sin of another, we forget how often and how deeply we have sinned, and that Jesus suffered the consequences for our sins. But when we remember our own sin, and we recall how Jesus carried our sin for us, we are more likely to allow Him to carry the sins of those who have sinned against us.

Giving the sins of others against us to Jesus to carry has a wonderful result: our burden is lightened, because when we carry sin of any kind, we are weighted down by that sin. Carrying the sins of another person, which is what we do when we do not forgive, is like wearing the chains of someone else's slavery. Forgiveness breaks those chains and frees us from their sin. Even more than the consequences of the actual sins of others against us, allowing those sins to bleed away our own joy and peace is much more damaging to us. Carrying a sin we did not commit, and is not ours to carry, is a heavy and unnecessary burden to bear.

The offender does not need to acknowledge their sin, to repent, or to ask for our forgiveness in order for us to forgive. Forgiveness happens between God and the forgiving person alone. In fact, carrying the sins of others, where we have no authority to do anything with or about the sin, leaves us feeling powerless and trapped.

Forgiveness, as defined by giving the sins of others against us into the hands of Jesus, frees us, places the sinner in the hands of the Lord Who can do something with the sin, and restores our peace and joy. "And forgive us our debts, as we also have forgiven our debtors" (Matthew 6:12).

We can adopt a frame of mind that includes gratitude, perseverance, contentment, acceptance, surrender, and forgiveness, even in the worst circumstances this life and the enemy offer up. Gratitude serves us well in our Desert of lack, reminding us of what we have instead of tempting us with what our flesh wants to have. Like Jesus, we will be able to withstand the enemy's temptations.

Perseverance helps us endure in our Egypt, our Wilderness, and our Babylon. If the Israelites had persevered, they could have entered the Promised Land a generation sooner. And we know what happened to Shadrach, Meshach, and Abednego when they persevered in Babylon: yes, they walked into the fiery furnace, but they were met there by the Lord, Who carried them through unscathed.

Contentment sustains us as we walk through the Valley of illness and the Gates of observing the suffering of someone we love, or the Gethsemane of anticipation of our own suffering. These circumstances lose power over our feelings, and we are able to relish our relationships and enjoy who we are with instead of allowing the enemy to rob the time we have.

Acceptance is the balm of the Lord in our Tomb of grief. It allows us to focus on Jesus instead of on our pain, and receive His comfort and healing. Surrender frees us to walk into our Berakah, where our enemies surround us, without fear, and to step out on the waves despite the Storm to meet the Lord, without doubt.

Forgiveness provides us escape from our Cave of isolation. We no longer need to protect ourselves from others by hiding our true selves away; instead, we can step out into the light and walk with the Lord in peace and joy.

As you walk in these perspectives, "May the God of hope fill you with all joy and peace as you trust in him, so that you may overflow with hope by the power of the Holy Spirit" (Romans 15:13).

Questions for Prayer

Now, we seek to adopt these perspectives in our hearts by asking the Lord for truth and listening for His responses to our questions. Our questions will explore the ideas presented in this section to insure their reliability, and will open us up to receive more truth that will continue to strengthen our stand. Remember, if you do not readily hear from the Lord, be patient with yourself and the process. Do not push to the point of frustration; extend yourself grace, take a break from listening when needed, move on from questions where you are getting stuck, and come back to those questions later.

Be sure to use your notebook to write down responses you receive from the Lord as you pray over each question. Don't trust your memory alone to retain every detail of what He shows you.

Lord, I ask that You would be with me as I seek to listen to Your voice and learn more about adopting a new framework for my life. Open my heart to receive Your truth, and guard my heart against the enemy's lies. Show me, Jesus...

1. What hindrances are in my life to having the fruits of Your Spirit of love, joy, and peace?

2. What is my current and usual frame of reference in response to circumstances in my life?

3. What are the things You would like for me to see with gratitude in my life?

4. Where would the perspective of perseverance most benefit me currently?

5. What are some examples in my life where discontentment is creating jealousy and dissatisfaction?

6. What are some things in my life I need to accept that I cannot change?

7. How can I best receive the seeds of truth You plant in my heart?

8. What are accurate ways to see those around me so I receive them as You receive them?

9. What are some things I am trying to control that I need to surrender to You?

10. Who and what do I need to forgive?

Meditations

Spend time contemplating the ideas presented below, always keeping your heart and mind open to the leading of the Lord. Refer to the Scriptures at the beginning of this section as you meditate on these truths. If you have questions about any of these concepts, turn to the Lord in prayer and ask Him for His understanding.

STRENGTH IN ADVERSITY

The mental framework I use to interpret my life, and the point of view or perspective from which I see my circumstances determines in large part how I am feeling in any given situation.

Like Paul, with Your help, I can be grateful and content in all my circumstances, no matter what those circumstances are. If I focus on where You focus my eyes, and take my eyes off worldly perspectives, gratitude and contentment will flow naturally from me.

Perseverance stands directly against Satan's attempt to entice me into the role of victim, while passivity reinforces a victim stance and encourages acquiescence to Satan's schemes and resignation to the whims of this world. Acceptance and surrender, on the other hand, are the wisdom and choice to release control.

When I receive truth from You, I will choose to accept Your truth completely in my heart and believe it wholly in my mind, allowing Your seeds of truth to be planted deeply, so they grow good fruit.

Forgiveness does not require an action or repentance from the one who sinned against me, nor does it demand I forget or excuse the offense or have a relationship with the offender. Forgiveness involves letting go of the sin against me and giving that sin to Jesus, trusting His justice and His care and love for me to handle that sin.

Process

Process these suggested areas of focus based on this section. Remember, the goal is for you to grasp concepts, not develop a list of steps to take or rules to follow. If you understand the concepts, you will be able to see the whole picture, and can better understand any of its parts and apply the information presented to your own life. These suggestions may not match concepts that you valued from this section, so add your own concepts, based on beliefs and attitudes you have chosen to adopt from the reading and your time with the Lord, and applications that work for you. Incorporate these concepts in your daily meditations and prayer. As you synthesize and apply these concepts, combine them with the concepts you learned in the previous sections. Practice recalling each concept during times of adversity, and applying the concepts, with the Lord's help.

Synthesis: I choose to "clothe" my mind in the perspectives of gratitude, perseverance, contentment, acceptance, surrender, and forgiveness.

Application: When I am in difficult circumstances:

I will focus on the good things I have in my life and thank the Lord for those things.

I will face the difficulty head on, and walk through it with the Lord as my partner.

I will rejoice in myself alone, not in comparison to others or seeking the approval of others, focusing instead on the Lord's unconditional approval of who I am.

I will accept the things I cannot change and change the things I am able to change, and I will trust God to show me the difference.

I will freely place my whole self in God's hands and trust His heart for me.

I will forgive those who have sinned against me by giving their sin to the Lord.

Synthesis: I choose to fix my eyes on You, not on my circumstances, and I choose to believe what You say to me in my heart and mind, not other voices or other perspectives.

Application: When faced with adversity:

I will open my heart and lower any walls or defenses I have put in place.

I will quiet my mind to be receptive to the Lord's voice alone.

I will persevere in listening for truth from the Lord.

I will immediately reject any thoughts contrary to the truth I have received from the Lord.

Conclusion

In Section Seven, we examined six perspectives to adopt as a frame of mind during adversity. Each of these perspectives, when clothing our thoughts, results in peace and joy in our feelings. Gratitude reminds us of what we have. Perseverance helps us to endure. Contentment sustains us. Acceptance calms and soothes us. Surrender frees us to walk with the Lord. Forgiveness releases us from the sin of others. These perspectives are integrally connected, supporting and strengthening our hearts and minds during adversity. We encourage you to continuously practice adopting these perspectives in your daily life. As you walk through the Valley, choose to focus your eyes only on the Lord and His truth. As you brave the Storm, choose to frame your thoughts with the perspectives that bring you joy and peace. Making His thoughts your thoughts is the most wonderful response to adversity of all.

Now that our thoughts are centered on Jesus and His truth, let's experience living in the Kingdom of God, right here and right now. We do not have to wait on heaven; Jesus promises us His Kingdom is within.

EIGHT

THE KINGDOM OF GOD

Scripture

Remember to take time to read each verse carefully and in depth, not by rote, and to consider their application to facing adversity. Look up each verse, and read several verses leading up to and following the selection to understand the context. Ask what the Lord is wanting to say to you as you read these verses.

Matthew 13:44-46 *"The kingdom of heaven is like treasure hidden in a field. When a man found it, he hid it again, and then in his joy went and sold all he had and bought that field. "Again, the kingdom of heaven is like a merchant looking for fine pearls. When he found one of great value, he went away and sold everything he had and bought it."*

Luke 17:20-21 *Once, on being asked by the Pharisees when the kingdom of God would come, Jesus replied, "The coming of the kingdom of God is not something that can be observed, nor will people say, 'Here it is,' or 'There it is,' because the kingdom of God is in your midst."*

Mark 10:14-15 *He said to them, "Let the little children come to me, and do not hinder them, for the kingdom of God belongs to such as these. Truly I tell you, anyone who will not receive the kingdom of God like a little child will never enter it."*

Matthew 25:1-10 *"At that time the kingdom of heaven will be like ten virgins who took their lamps and went out to meet the bridegroom. Five of them were foolish and five were wise. The foolish ones took their lamps but did not take any oil with them. The wise ones, however, took oil in jars along with their lamps. The bridegroom was a long time in coming, and they all became drowsy and fell asleep. At midnight the cry rang out: 'Here's the bridegroom! Come out to meet him!' Then all the virgins woke up and trimmed their lamps. The foolish ones said to the wise, 'Give us some of your oil; our lamps are going out.' 'No,' they replied, 'there may not be enough for both us and you. Instead, go to those who sell oil and buy some for yourselves.' But while they were on their way to buy the oil, the bridegroom arrived. The virgins who were ready went in with him to the wedding banquet. And the door was shut.*

II Corinthians 4:6, 18 *For God, who said, "Let light shine out of darkness," made his light shine in our hearts to give us the light of the knowledge of God's glory displayed in the face of Christ. So, we fix our eyes not on what is seen, but on what is unseen, since what is seen is temporary, but what is unseen is eternal.*

John 17:22-23, 26 *"I have given them the glory that you gave me, that they may be one as we are one— I in them and you in me— so that they may be brought to complete unity. I have made you known to them, and will continue to make you known in order that the love you have for me may be in them and that I myself may be in them."*

Matthew 6:19-21 *"Do not store up for yourselves treasures on earth, where moths and vermin destroy, and where thieves break in and steal. But store up for yourselves treasures in heaven, where moths and vermin do not destroy, and where thieves do not break in and steal. For where your treasure is, there your heart will be also.*

The Kingdom Within

Jesus taught His disciples that the Kingdom of God was present in their here-and-now, and the Kingdom of God was within them. He was not focused on a future place; He centered His teaching on the Kingdom around His presence. Because of Christ's resurrection, these teachings are true for us as well. The Kingdom of God is within us, if He is present within us. "Now it is God who makes both us and you stand firm in Christ. He anointed us, set his seal of ownership on us, and put his Spirit in our hearts as a deposit, guaranteeing what is to come" (II Corinthians 1:21-22).

Just as Jesus brought God's Kingdom to this world when He came (Matthew 4:17), in the same way, He brings God's Kingdom when He enters our hearts, and our hearts become His Temple. When we experience our lives in His presence, we are living in the Kingdom of God, right here and right now.

In His presence. Living in the presence of Jesus means focusing on Him always and in all things, our eyes "fixed" on what is unseen and eternal instead of on what our physical senses

135

perceive. Living in His presence also means living in the moment, being fully present where we are with what we are doing, and being fully who we are in the here and now. These two concepts are inseparable; for we cannot be fully present if we are not in His presence, and we cannot be fully in His presence unless we are completely present and wholly ourselves. Psalm 16:8, 11 expresses this truth beautifully: "I keep my eyes always on the Lord. With him at my right hand, I will not be shaken. You make known to me the path of life; you will fill me with joy in your presence, with eternal pleasures at your right hand."

So, how do we live in the presence of the Lord? First, we need to know this truth: He is with us always, as He promised He would be, so the choice to be present with Him is ours. We can choose what we attend to and where we place our focus. Our physical senses are inundated by the worldly perspective, but we have a choice as to where we will "fix" our eyes and what we hear with our ears. We also need to truly understand God's grace, His mercy, and His love.

God's love is like a symphony. When we are listening to a beautiful piece of music performed at the highest level of ability, the music inundates us; it vibrates in our core and touches the deep places in our hearts. In the same way, the music of God's love surrounds us, moves through us and in us, and is for us. It is full and rich and glorious. Nothing can interrupt it. We can change our experience of His music by plugging our ears, screaming at the top of our lungs, or letting it be drowned out by distractions, but none of this changes the music or stops it from playing. We cannot change the music of His love.

Paul teaches us to "clothe" ourselves with Jesus Christ (Romans 13:14, Galatians 3:27) and with His nature of "compassion, kindness, humility, gentleness, and patience"

(Colossians 3:12). Unlike the spiritual warfare verses that tell us to "put on" the armor of God, as in don a garment, these verses have a connotation of full immersion. The language here describes being engulfed, as we would sink down into a warm, comfy bed and swaddle ourselves in a thick, soft blanket.

God's mercy is that infinite cushion, the place of rest for our souls (Matthew 11:29), catching us gently so our hearts do not crash and shatter beyond repair. As Paul describes it, "We are hard pressed on every side, but not crushed; perplexed, but not in despair; persecuted, but not abandoned; struck down, but not destroyed" (II Corinthians 4:8-9). He catches our sin and absorbs it onto Himself, alleviating the shame and restoring our connection with Him. He cushions our suffering and our loss in the softness of redemption. He lets us down gently from our mistakes, our failings, our blindness, and our confusion, so nothing is beyond recovery.

God's grace is that everlasting blanket, completely enveloping us and holding us close to His heart. His blanket is warm, inviting, soft, and complete; nothing is left exposed. Wrapped in His blanket, we can be at peace; we are cuddled like a small child against our loving Father's chest. It is our respite from the world. The outside of His blanket is thick and strong, a shield deflecting enemy arrows, keeping our spirits safe from harm and protecting us from fear.

However, instead of clothing ourselves in Christ, we try to manufacture our own "resting place" (Isaiah 28:12). "We have made a lie our refuge and falsehood our hiding place" (Isaiah 28:15). We are warned, "hail will sweep away your refuge, the lie, and water will overflow your hiding place. Your covenant with death will be annulled; your agreement with the realm of the dead will not stand. When the overwhelming scourge sweeps by, you will be beaten down by it. As often as it comes it will carry you away;

morning after morning, by day and by night, it will sweep through. The understanding of this message will bring sheer terror" (Isaiah 28:17-19). Still, we try to hide in our own bed under our own blanket, but "the bed is too short to stretch out on, the blanket too narrow to wrap around you" (Isaiah 28:20).

Despite our self-reliance, our self-focus, and our self-protection, Jesus will never leave us alone. We can't hide from Him (Psalm 139:7). Jesus is the living water that overflows our hiding places. He brings with Him a hail of truth to destroy the walls we build around our hearts, and He floods the isolation we buy for ourselves with His love.

Yes, we have a choice. We can keep on hiding. He still stays with us. We can avoid and run away. He still runs beside us. The main consequence of our hiding is we miss experiencing His love, even though nothing can separate us from it (Romans 8:39). Knowing the consequences, though, and being given a choice, doesn't it make more sense to choose Him as our refuge (Psalm 18:2); someone we can run to instead of away from, someone to hold us and cover us when our bed is too short and our covers are too narrow? His grace, mercy, and love are more than enough.

In play therapy, one method, called Developmental Play, proposes that anything external to the relationship between the child and the counselor is superfluous and distracting. Thus, all toys and other objects are removed from the play area. Instead of focusing on toys or games, the counselor and child focus completely on each other. Together, they create playful interactions using their combined imaginations. The relationship between the two grows and deepens, as their attachment to each other is created in the play.

We need "Developmental Play" with Jesus. When we put aside the distractions of the world, what our physical senses respond to, and our circumstances, we can truly focus on Emmanuel, God with us. He has imagined a story for us to share; together, we can begin to create the story we imagine together.

Nothing external to His presence in our hearts and our spirits joined with His, and all that is created in that union, is part of His Kingdom. The true evidence of us living in the Kingdom of God is, in fact, when the external no longer has power in our lives, because, in the Kingdom, circumstances no longer have power over us. Circumstances do not determine what we believe, how we feel, or what we choose. Instead, in the Kingdom, our oneness with God leads us. His voice alone has authority in our lives. His is the only voice we listen to.

Much in the same way that the setting of a play can be elaborate or it can be sparse, but our eyes are focused on the actors and their interaction, our circumstances can be pleasant or they can be difficult, but our relationship with Jesus remains our central focal point. He always remains the same, providing stability and grounding, as He becomes the anchor for our souls (Hebrews 6:19). His presence and His truth are the stable and sure things in our lives; the things that are eternal, not transient and temporary.

Just like Stephen, whose eyes were fixed on heaven opening and the glory of the Lord shining forth and Jesus standing at the right hand of God, but who did not see the stones raining down on his head (Acts 7:55-56), we can live with our eyes on the Lord, and our circumstances will fade into the background. Living in this truth is living in the Kingdom of God.

To help us focus on the presence of Jesus, we can apply a variety of practices. We can surround ourselves with truth, love and beauty, staying away from negativity and the worldly facets of life opposed to God's views. We can place constant reminders in our surroundings to keep our thoughts on His truth, such as symbolic images representing specific truths we have received from the Lord,

Scripture verses or phrases and meaningful sayings displayed in key locations we frequent, and sticky notes on mirrors and the refrigerator door highlighting key elements of God's nature or our own.

We can write new insights received from the Lord in a "truth journal" each day, and review these writings frequently. We can discipline ourselves to stop indulging in sin-based behaviors and lie-based thoughts, actively rejecting them before they are internalized in us. We can speak truth to ourselves and aloud to others, so that our ears are reminded continuously of that truth we know from Him. But above all, the most critical aspect of living in His presence involves centering our attention on Him, talking to Him, listening to His responses, and watching His actions and reactions.

As Jesus said, He only did what He saw the Father doing (John 5:19). He is in the Father and the Father is in Him (John 14:10). Jesus goes on to enjoin us to remain in His love (John 15:9) and to pray that we would be in Him as He is in the Father and the Father is in Him (John 17:21). From these teachings of Jesus, we can see that it is both possible and preferable that we remain "in Him" as He was with His Father, focused only on what His Father was doing and saying.

To live in this manner means choosing to pray without ceasing, as we are taught by Paul to do (I Thessalonians 5:17): prayer defined as an ongoing, two-way, and intimate conversation with the Lord, where we ask Him for truth in all circumstances, where we take the time to listen, where we trust His direction and guidance, and where we allow Him to pour out His love in our hearts. Self-reliance, self-protection, self-criticism, self-deprecation, self-pity, self-centeredness, self-judgment, self-promotion, and even self-esteem are all examples of looking to ourselves instead of to Jesus, and we cannot look to both at the same time.

We tend not to think about His presence with us until we run into something we believe we can't handle. By then, the enemy has already blown apart our feeble defenses and consumed our minds and hearts. In responding in this way, we are excluding the Lord, Who is standing right with us, within us, desiring to take our hands and walk with us through each and every moment of our day. We are also denying our identity, because our identity is in His identity. He is in us, and we are in Him. We "are being transformed into his image with ever-increasing glory" (II Corinthians 3:18).

The Kingdom is like. Jesus likens the Kingdom of God to a treasure or a priceless pearl, worth selling everything to possess. What is Jesus saying to us in this parable? We might think Jesus is referring to the value of the future place we will go, at a future time, as if He is teaching us to focus now on going to heaven later; however, the actions taken in this parable are immediate and in the present. The man sold all he had and bought the field so he owned the treasure. The merchant sold everything he had and bought the pearl of greatest value, right then and right there.

What if the treasure and pearl is hidden within us? Our greatest gift and our most valuable treasure is the aspect of the nature of God that He made a part of our identity at our creation. This identity may be "hidden" from us for a time, but if we search for it, with His help, we will find it. Selling everything else we own to have our true identity means letting go of all of the old values, old beliefs, and old ways that have hidden our true selves. It means allowing Him to take down the walls and remove the masks we've used for a false sense of safety.

The treasure of your true identity is within you now, perhaps long hidden; or, perhaps you have some awareness of its presence. Imagine taking a beautiful, priceless, one-of-a-kind jewel, like a flawless pearl, and using that jewel to buy an unnecessary plastic object at the dollar store. You would never consider doing such a thing!!! Would you?

Consider this: you may be doing the equivalent right now. Without realizing the value of what God has given you, the treasure of who you are, you may be trading it in to the enemy in exchange for a few cheap thrills, a momentary pleasure, the acceptance or approval of others, the illusion of control, a covering for your shame, a false self-image, a sense of power or status, or similar things which are of no benefit or gain in the Kingdom perspective. You may be cluttering up your "house" with a whole lot of dollar store fluff, while ignoring the presence and love of Jesus.

Have you so devalued your own priceless pearl within you that you willingly trade it in for the spangle and glitz of Satan's feeble offerings? You only need to seek your true identity, ask Jesus to help you to release those things you have purchased in its place, and claim what is God-given in order to have the greatest treasure of all.

Jesus also compares living in the Kingdom of God to being ready for the Bridegroom, with enough oil in our lamps to make it through until He comes. In this parable, the oil for their lamps refers to the presence of God's Spirit, providing light in times of darkness. The wedding banquet refers to the Kingdom within us now.

The five wise virgins were prepared; they brought the Spirit of the Living God with them to fill them and light their way through the darkness or time of adversity. They had already developed that strength of relationship, by focusing on their relationship with God as the thing of primary importance. They had invested their resources wisely into that relationship, instead of spending their time, energy, and resources on other things, whatever worldly things might try to distract from their relationship with God and His presence within their hearts. They were ready when the time of deepest darkness came.

The five foolish virgins, however, were not ready. They brought their lamps; in other words, they knew the Bridegroom was coming, meaning they knew about Jesus, but they failed to invest in the oil for their lamp, the intimate presence of the Holy Spirit.

Although five were prepared and five were not, they all dozed off. Just like the disciples who could not stay awake with Jesus at Gethsemane, no matter how deeply we love Jesus, we can still succumb to the weakness of the flesh, and can "fall asleep" when things seem to be going along fine in our lives.

Suddenly, the Bridegroom is approaching and the alarm is sounding, and the five foolish virgins become aware they are not prepared. Notice that the preparation of the five wise virgins is not going to be enough to cover the five foolish virgins; it can only provide oil enough for their own lamps. In other words, their relationship with Jesus cannot sustain others during their time of adversity. We each need our own oil to make it through those times.

Jesus is giving us an important warning here: prepare by investing in your relationship with God as of first importance, for when the time of adversity comes, you will not be able to stand in the light without that preparation to sustain you, and you cannot rely on the relationship of others with Jesus to sustain you.

We cannot serve two masters. We cannot have two "gods." Jesus said, "Either you will hate the one and love the other, or you will be devoted to the one and despise the other" (Matthew 6:24). We cannot stand with one foot in the Kingdom and the other in the world, nor can we focus on our relationship with Jesus as the thing of primary importance while focusing on things of the worldly view as equally, or even more, important to us. Whatever the foolish virgins were doing with their resources, they were not investing in that connection with Jesus through the presence of the Holy Spirit within. They were counting on what they had in the lamp already to see them through adversity. It will not be enough.

At some point, all of us will face adversity. We may experience our own Egypt, in the form of slavery to a destructive behavior or belief, or the bondage of feeling powerless and trapped in our circumstances. Our heart's desires may seem permanently out of reach, or we may feel cut off and distant from God in our own type of Wilderness. We may face an overwhelming trial, our own fire to walk through like the Israelite men in Babylon. The enemy may attack us from all sides, and pile on more and more hardship when we are already down, like at Berakah.

All of us will walk through the Valley of illness and the Tomb of grief, because no one can escape the inevitable deterioration of what Paul calls this "earthly tent" (II Corinthians 5:1). We also will all stand at the Gates, watching those we love suffering; at Gethsemane, fearing our own suffering; and, at Calvary, suffering because of the actions or choices of someone else.

We may face a Storm of chaos and doubt, a Cave of isolation and loneliness, or a Desert of lack where the temptation to fill ourselves with something other than God is strongest. Wherever we are, whatever we are experiencing, no matter what circumstances come our way, and whatever arrows the enemy fires at us, there is one constant. The presence of Jesus Christ, filling our hearts with His Kingdom, sustains us, strengthens us, and carries us through it all.

Questions for Prayer

Now, we seek to live in the Kingdom in our hearts and recover the treasure of our true identity by asking the Lord for truth and listening for His responses to our questions. Our questions will explore the ideas presented in this section to insure their reliability, and will open us up to receive more truth that will continue to deepen our relationship with Jesus. Remember, if you do not readily hear from the Lord, be patient with yourself and the process. Do not push to the point of frustration; extend yourself grace, take a break from listening when needed, move on from questions where you are getting stuck, and come back to those questions later.

Be sure to use your notebook to write down responses you receive from the Lord as you pray over each question. Don't trust your memory alone to retain every detail of what He shows you.

Lord, I ask that You would be with me as I seek to listen to Your voice and learn more about Your Kingdom within, in the here and now. Open my heart to receive Your truth, and guard my heart against the enemy's lies. Show me, Jesus…

1. What did You mean when You said, "the Kingdom of God is in your midst"?

2. What are some ways I have "fixed" my eyes on what is seen and temporal, and not on the unseen and eternal?

3. In what ways am I drowning out the symphony of Your love?

4. What helps me to rest my soul in the cushion of Your mercy?

5. What does it mean to be engulfed in the blanket of Your grace?

6. What would it look like if You and I were doing spiritual Developmental Play together?

7. What are some methods I can use each day to focus on Your constant presence with me?

8. What do I need to sell for me to purchase the treasure of the Kingdom within me?

9. What clutter do I need to get rid of to possess the pearl of my true identity?

10. What are some things I can do to fill the oil in my lamp so I am prepared for coming adversity?

Meditations

Spend time contemplating the ideas presented below, always keeping your heart and mind open to the leading of the Lord. Refer to the Scriptures at the beginning of this section as you meditate on these truths. If you have questions about any of these concepts, turn to the Lord in prayer and ask Him for His understanding.

The Kingdom of God is within me, because You make Your home in my heart. I am not waiting for some future place to experience Your Kingdom; I can live in Your Kingdom, right here and right now, as I focus on Your presence and recognize You are always with me.

My own bed of rest is too short for me, and my own blanket of safety is too narrow to cover me; however, Your love, grace, and mercy are sufficient. As You flood my hiding place, break down my walls, and destroy my lies, I am engulfed in Your love, and I will find rest for my soul.

My circumstances fade into the background, and become a setting where I experience my relationship with You instead of my all-consuming focus, when I am one with You as You are One with the Father. My identity is in Your identity as I am transformed into Your image.

I have exchanged my identity for the offerings of a cheap thrill or momentary pleasure, acceptance and approval from others, the illusion of control or worldly power, and a hiding place to cover my shame and my fear. These offerings are from the enemy. I want to sell these unnecessary things and purchase Your Kingdom within.

To be prepared to stand in strength during adversity, I need Your Spirit to fill me completely. Simply knowing about You is not enough. I must make our relationship my highest priority, and fully invest in our relationship, if I hope to have enough "oil" in my lamp to sustain me.

Process

Process these suggested areas of focus based on this section. Remember, the goal is for you to grasp concepts, not develop a list of steps to take or rules to follow. If you understand the concepts, you will be able to see the whole picture, and can better understand any of its parts and apply the information presented to your own life. These suggestions may not match concepts that you valued from this section, so add your own concepts, based on beliefs and attitudes you have chosen to adopt from the reading and your time with the Lord, and applications that work for you. Incorporate these concepts in your daily meditations and prayer. As you synthesize and apply these concepts, combine them with the concepts you learned in the previous sections. Practice recalling each concept during times of adversity, and applying the concepts, with the Lord's help.

Synthesis: I choose to listen only to the symphony of Your love, sink deeply into the cushion of Your mercy, and allow You to engulf me in the blanket of Your grace.

Application: Each day from now on:

I will free my mind from negativity and worldly inputs.

I will surround myself with visual cues and symbols of the Lord's love and His truth.

I will keep a truth journal, where I write down truth received from the Lord, and I will reread the journal on a regular basis.

I will speak truth, both in my head and aloud to myself and others.

I will play with the Lord, and in that process, imagine and create a new story with Him.

Synthesis: I choose to reject the cheap offerings of the enemy, and purchase the Kingdom within, investing fully in my relationship with You.

Application: As I prepare for adversity:

I will ask the Lord to show me the true nature of what I have "bought" in exchange for His presence.

I will allow the Lord to remove all clutter from my heart.

I will demonstrate the Kingdom is my priority by spending time, energy, and focus on the Lord and on deepening my relationship with Him.

I will listen to the Lord and believe what He says to me, rejecting all other concepts, perceptions, and beliefs.

I will ask the Lord to transform me into His image, and make His identity my identity.

Conclusion

In Section Eight, we discussed the Kingdom of God within us in the here-and-now, and living in the presence of Jesus. We looked at the sufficiency of God's love, mercy, and grace, as compared to our own efforts at rest and safety. Living in the Kingdom now means immersing ourselves constantly in Jesus' presence, and allowing His love, mercy, and grace to engulf us. Jesus likened the Kingdom to a treasure and a priceless pearl, and compared living in the Kingdom to adequately preparing for adversity by filling our lamps with the Holy Spirit. These analogies point us toward clothing ourselves in Christ. We encourage you to continuously invest in your relationship with Jesus in your daily life, making His presence your first priority. As you walk through the Valley, choose to focus your eyes only on the Lord and His truth. As you brave the Storm, choose to discard all enemy clutter and allow Jesus to transform you into His image. The presence of Jesus in our hearts is the one constant through all adversity. His presence sustains us.

As this journey draws to its conclusion, remember that living in the Kingdom and deepening our relationship with Jesus is a process of continuous investment, growth, and transformation. Toward that end, let's synthesize all the sections and apply what we have learned and experienced toward strengthening ourselves to face adversity.

CONCLUSION

FIX OUR EYES

Scripture

Hebrews 3:1 *Therefore, holy brothers and sisters, who share in the heavenly calling, fix your thoughts on Jesus.*

Hebrews 3:6 *Christ is faithful as the Son over God's house. And we are his house, if indeed we hold firmly to our confidence and the hope in which we glory.*

Hebrews 3:12-13 *See to it, brothers and sisters, that none of you has a sinful, unbelieving heart that turns away from the living God. But encourage one another daily, as long as it is called "Today," so that none of you may be hardened by sin's deceitfulness.*

Hebrews 4:1-2 *Therefore, since the promise of entering his rest still stands, let us be careful that none of you be found to have fallen short of it. For we also have had the good news proclaimed to us, just as they did; but the message they heard was of no value to them, because they did not share the faith of those who obeyed.*

(Some manuscripts say: *because those who heard did not combine it with faith.*)

Hebrews 4:11 *Let us, therefore, make every effort to enter that rest, so that no one will perish.*

Hebrews 4:12-16 *For the word of God is alive and active. Sharper than any double-edged sword, it penetrates even to dividing soul and spirit, joints and marrow; it judges the thoughts and attitudes of the heart. Nothing in all creation is hidden from God's sight. Everything is uncovered and laid bare before the eyes of him to whom we must give account. Therefore, since we have a great high priest who has ascended into heaven, Jesus the Son of God, let us hold firmly to the faith we profess. For we do not have a high priest who is unable to empathize with our weaknesses, but we have one who has been tempted in every way, just as we are—yet he did not sin. Let us then approach God's throne of grace with confidence, so that we may receive mercy and find grace to help us in our time of need.*

Hebrews 5:13-14 *Anyone who lives on milk, being still an infant, is not acquainted with the teaching about righteousness. But solid food is for the mature, who by constant use have trained themselves to distinguish good from evil.*

Hebrews 6:11-12 *We want each of you to show this same diligence to the very end, so that what you hope for may be fully realized. We do not want you to become lazy, but to imitate those who through faith and patience inherit what has been promised.*

Hebrews 12:1-3 Therefore, since we are surrounded by such a great cloud of witnesses, let us throw off everything that hinders and the sin that so easily entangles. And let us run with perseverance the race marked out for us, fixing our eyes on Jesus, the pioneer and perfecter of faith. For the joy set before him he endured the cross, scorning its shame, and sat down at the right hand of the throne of God. Consider him who endured such opposition from sinners, so that you will not grow weary and lose heart.

Putting It All Together

As you can tell from the list of Scripture for our conclusion, we are taking a journey through the book of Hebrews as our foundation for the synthesis and application of the concepts presented during this journey. The writer of Hebrews does an excellent job of delineating the key points of faith for a disciple of Christ, so it is fitting this book would serve as a focal point for drawing together the main ideas from each section.

The writer of Hebrews provides us with a simple and straightforward direction: "fix your thoughts on Jesus." These are our marching orders; in other words, our instructions for how to walk out each day. Let's look at the meaning of this simple direction.

To "fix" is to make fast, firm, and stable; to direct steadily and to hold there permanently; to set immovable in one place and not waver. For many of us, we allow our thoughts to wander away from Jesus into other areas, including looking backward into the past, imagining forward into the future, and focusing on ourselves or our circumstances in the present. We allow the ideas and beliefs that are opposed to Jesus to dominate our thinking, and we entertain the interjected thoughts of the enemy, even knowing they do not match the truth of God. How, then, can we follow this simple instruction?

Christ is faithful. At the outset, we need to accept that we cannot fulfill this instruction on our own. It may seem like a circular argument to say we need Jesus in order to fix our thoughts on Jesus, but accepting this truth is the beginning of actually following the directive given in Hebrews. If we truly know we need Jesus, even to follow this simple and straightforward teaching, we are much more likely to include Jesus in all our thoughts and actions, thus ultimately fulfilling the direction we are given. Remember the boy's father who exclaimed in response to Jesus, "I do believe; help me overcome my unbelief." (Mark 9:24).

Once we accept we need Jesus' help to keep our thoughts fixed on Him, we need to continually recenter ourselves with Him by asking moment by moment for His input into our daily living. If we truly see Jesus as our partner and friend, our constant companion, and the loving parent to our child, we are much more likely to turn to Him as we make choices, and to remember that He is with us in every circumstance we experience.

Think about a truly loving parent with a small child: every little action of their child is captivating to the parent; everything learned is a delight, and every experience meaningful; every question asked is thoughtfully addressed. Just like a good parent, nothing in our lives is beyond His caring; nothing is insignificant, because of His love for us. Through knowing these truths, and with the gentle help of our loving Father, we can keep our thoughts fixed on Jesus.

We also need to remember our heart is His home, and care for ourselves in alignment with that truth. He lives within us, and He never leaves us. Our best interests are at the center of His will.

Living in accord with who He says we are is the best way to live in His presence and express our love for Him. How we treat ourselves in all areas of our lives needs to reflect our value in His eyes.

Guard your heart. As a follow-up to the instruction to "fix" our thoughts on Jesus, the writer of Hebrews has a warning for our hearts: do not let your heart be hardened by lies because the result will be turning away from God. As is stated several other places in Scripture (John 1:14-17, John 3:21, John 8:32, John 14:6, John 16:13, I Corinthians 13:6, Ephesians 4:14-15, Ephesians 5:9, Ephesians 6:14, I Timothy 3:9, I Peter 1:22, I John 3:18-20), the truth is something that is of highest value. It is meant to be guarded and held in our hearts. These are just a sample of the many Scriptures that express the priceless value of truth.

At the same time, Scripture is filled with warnings against anything that opposes the truth (John 8:44, Acts 20:30, Romans 1:18, Romans 2:8, Galatians 5:7, II Thessalonians 2:9-10, Hebrews 10:26, I John 1:6). Again, these are just a sampling of Scriptures that warn us against believing lies and letting go of the truth. So, Scripture is clear we are to value the truth of God above anything else we might hear, anything we may believe, and anything we feel. We are to reject anything that is not in accord with the truth we have received from Him.

This warning from the writer of Hebrews is not a casual "oh, by the way, you might want to consider" type of warning. It is a life or death warning, because to turn away from God is death. So, begin by separating all lies from His truth in your heart. This exercise is the essence of discernment, which comes as a gift from the Holy Spirit. Resolve to listen only to His truth, and ask Jesus to strengthen you heart and your faith to believe only His truth, and to reject all lies from the enemy. The enemy's three lies are judgment, shame, and fear. Listen to your internal and spoken language as an aid in recognizing when a lie is present.

Once you have received a base of truth from Jesus, from that point forward, evaluate what you hear, believe, and feel against the truth you know. Anything that does not match or agree with the truth in your heart as revealed by the Holy Spirit, reject immediately. "Take captive every thought to make it obedient to Christ" (II Corinthians 10:5). Do not consider or entertain it; do not try it out in your heart; do not internalize it; do not be deceived by the enemy's attempts to veil it or put bows on it to make it attractive. Remember, all the so-called "gifts" of the enemy are bitter poison, no matter how sweet they look at the start. Remember also the warning given by the writer of Hebrews: do not remain in sin and lies lest your heart be hardened and you turn away from the living God (Hebrews 4:6-7).

Enter His rest. Next, the writer of Hebrews focuses on entering God's rest. As a context, the writer is drawing a comparison between the Israelites who, having been freed from Egypt, did not believe God and were therefore left to wander in the wilderness for forty years. To enter His rest means to enter the Promised Land.

We, too, have been freed from bondage by Christ. So, what is our "Promised Land"? The writer is referring to the Kingdom of God within our hearts. As Jesus taught, "anyone who will not receive the kingdom of God like a little child will never enter it" (Mark 10:15), referencing receiving in full His Kingdom within us by returning to our created identity, the writer of Hebrews is pointing us back to entering into the presence of Jesus within our hearts, so we do not miss experiencing the Kingdom here-and-now.

Remember, separation from God is perishing. Don't be deceived to think you have received what Jesus offers in full simply by receiving the good news. According to the writer of Hebrews, receiving the good news and combining it with faith; in other words, receiving it as a little child, with full belief, acceptance, utter dependency, and hope; allows you to enter His rest. Without faith, we are still acting as "god" of our own lives, attempting to control circumstances, managing things on our own, protecting and defending ourselves, judging how it "should" be, and working to make everything like we want it to be. All that effort is exhausting, anxiety-provoking, and futile, because in truth, we don't have control over anything. There will be no peace, and no rest, for us.

Therefore, just as a tiny child focuses on their parents as the deepest objects of their love, center your mind and heart on the presence of Jesus. He is your first love, your only source, your one certainty, and the only one you can trust with your heart without hesitation or doubt. Then and only then will you enter His rest.

Partner with Christ. Now, the writer goes on to explain why we need to fix our thoughts specifically on Jesus. We first need to remember that the Word of God refers to Jesus, not to the Bible. "The Word became flesh and made his dwelling among us. We have seen his glory, the glory of the one and only Son, who came from the Father, full of grace and truth" (John 1:14). So, the writer is telling us the living Christ is active in our lives, penetrating to divide soul and spirit, and seeing clearly the thoughts and attitudes of our hearts.

Notice two key elements here in the description of Christ: first, it states He divides our soul (our emotions, thoughts, memories, etc.) from our spirit (our created being in God, made in His image) in much the same way He divides what is external (joints) from what is internal (marrow), and what is good and right and true (of the Kingdom) from everything else (of the world); and, second, He does not judge our actions or behaviors, He looks upon the deep places within us and sees the truth of our hearts.

As much as we try to hide from others or from ourselves, our obfuscation and denial cannot withstand His piercing eyes. Therefore, if we want to live in truth, being who He made us to be and living in His Kingdom in the here and now, we need to be consumed in Christ, our eyes seeing only Him.

The writer talks about how Jesus empathizes with our weaknesses, having been tempted in the same ways we are tempted daily. All things are possible through joining with Jesus in partnership. He pulls the Lion's share of the load, for as He said, "Come to me, all you who are weary and burdened, and I will give you rest. Take my yoke upon you and learn from me, for I am gentle and humble in heart, and you will find rest for your souls. For my yoke is easy and my burden is light" (Matthew 11:28-30).

We can approach God with confidence because we come with Christ. We can live from our spirits, with our spirits fully expressed and reigning over our souls, because of Christ. We can see through the eyes of truth, because we can see through the eyes of Christ. Everything we are, and everything we can have, is because of Christ.

Spiritual maturity. As the writer of Hebrews continues to point us toward fixing our thoughts on Jesus, he calls us into a deeper relationship with God, one that goes beyond the "milk" of believing in God and repenting of sin. Those things are important and necessary, but the spiritually mature go well beyond these foundational truths. The writer refers to two elements of maturity: righteousness, and distinguishing good from evil. What does he mean when he refers to the "teaching about righteousness"?

Jesus taught many things about righteousness, best summarized in the verse, "But seek first his kingdom and his righteousness, and all these things will be given to you as well" (Matthew 6:33). From this verse, we see that Jesus connects seeking His Kingdom with righteousness.

Paul also talks a lot about righteousness; for example, in Philippians 3:9, he teaches how our righteousness comes from God. In Romans 6:13, Paul writes, "Do not offer any part of yourself to sin as an instrument of wickedness, but rather offer yourselves to God as those who have been brought from death to life; and offer every part of yourself to him as an instrument of righteousness." We see here the connection between surrendering to God and righteousness. Do you see how closely tied together the idea of fixing our eyes and thoughts on Jesus is with living in the Kingdom here-and-now within us, which is living in righteousness? According to the writer of Hebrews, this is spiritual maturity.

In addition, being able to distinguish good from evil indicates the presence of spiritual maturity. Someone who does not recognize evil for what it is, or who claims there is only good and denies the reality of the enemy of God, has not "trained themselves" to distinguish good from evil, and will not see the subtle and cunning machinations of the enemy, leaving themselves open to being easily caught in his traps. If we are not forewarned, we are not forearmed. As Isaiah prophesied, "Woe to those who call evil good and good evil, who put darkness for light and light for darkness, who put bitter for sweet and sweet for bitter. Woe to those who are wise in their own eyes and clever in their own sight." (Isaiah 5:20-21).

Once more, we see we are to be in constant communication with Christ and not rely on ourselves alone to distinguish good and evil, for discernment is a gift of the Holy Spirit. We rely on Him to show us the difference, and to reveal what is hidden and to bring out into the open what is concealed (Mark 4:22). Only by fixing our thoughts and eyes on Christ will we truly come into spiritual maturity.

Finish the race. In chapters 6-11, the writer of Hebrews focuses our attention on the truths of the redeeming blood of Christ, and the definition of faith, toward moving us into spiritual maturity, which is marked by the righteousness of Christ evidenced in us and the ability to discern good from evil. Then, the writer returns to his main point and instruction: to run the race with perseverance by fixing our eyes on Jesus.

With the ability to discern good from evil comes the ability to choose to "throw off" (Hebrews 12:1) those things that are not of God, like we are shucking off an old, ratty coat. He acknowledges sin is a snare, and it is easy to get trapped. He points out, Jesus endured opposition, and even Jesus was tempted. But he is emphasizing that we have a choice. We can choose to focus on Jesus and Jesus alone. Because Jesus is the originator of our faith, and the only one who can perfect our faith, we always have access to His power and strength to help us to stand against evil.

As Paul writes, "Stand firm, then, and do not let yourselves be burdened again by a yoke of slavery" (Galatians 5:1); and, "Finally, be strong in the Lord and in his mighty power. Put on the full armor of God, so that you can take your stand against the devil's schemes. For our struggle is not against flesh and blood, but against the rulers, against the authorities, against the powers of this dark world and against the spiritual forces of evil in the heavenly realms" (Ephesians 6:10-12).

As we walk through Valley and Storm, through Desert and Wilderness, and through fire and battle, at the end of the day, we want to be able to say, "I have fought the good fight, I have finished the race, I have kept the faith" (II Timothy 4:7). The only thing that could keep us from running our race with perseverance is our own choice, for Jesus has done His part. He has sought us. He has redeemed us. He loves us with all His heart. Now, only our choice remains. Where will I choose to fix my eyes? Who, or what, will dominate my thoughts? Choosing Jesus as the answer to these questions every day, through the strength and authority given to us by Christ, is our strength to stand in adversity.

Footnotes

[1]Lewis, C. S. (1952). *Mere Christianity.* New York: Harper Collins.

[2]The Andy Griffith Show (1961). *Opie and the Bully.* Season 2, Episode 1.

[3]Shapiro, Fred R. (2014). *Who wrote the Serenity Prayer?* The Chronicle Review.

[4]Lane, D. E. and Lane, H. J. (2007), *Restored Christianity (1st Edition).* Portland, OR: Inkwater Press.

MORE TITLES BY THESE AUTHORS

Strength in our Story is an 8-week Bible study of the story of Joseph, designed to help you discover healing and hope in life's darkest moments. Through these materials, individuals gain context for life experiences and events, find healing, and build God-focused communities. A Facilitator Guide and Participant Manual are available.

The Interview takes you on one woman's transformational journey through the challenges, pitfalls, and complexities of spiritual warfare. Satan and Jesus square off over the young woman, who is struggling to cope with her traumatic past.

Wilderness Meditations is a book of devotions for reading and study during the 40 days of Lent. The focus of the devotions is on discovering the nature of God, developing an intimate, personal connection with Jesus, deepening your prayer life, and gaining a greater understanding of truth. Each devotion includes a theme for meditation for that day, all centering on the character of Christ.

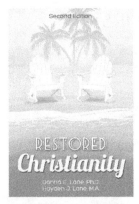

Restored Christianity integrates historical analysis with an in-depth examination of the current state of Christian belief toward restoring the earliest known, foundational beliefs of Christianity. Using Paul's letters, the authors confront current beliefs about such topics as the nature of God, the mysteries of God, the intention and use of the Bible, the meaning of faith, the sovereignty of God, our purpose, suffering, and the efficacy of prayer.

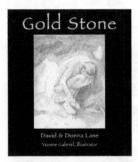

Gold Stone tells the story of young Caonaciba, who is dealing with the annihilation of his family and community at the hand of early discoverers of the New World. Caonaciba faces his grief with the help of three guides, who remind the young boy of his identity and help him to begin his new life.

Please Share the Door, I'm Freezing is a marriage workbook designed to help couples create the oneness in their marriage that God desires. Topics include God's basic elements for a happy marriage, identifying and removing beliefs that create division, praying together effectively, submitting to each other in love, living in peace, becoming allies instead of adversaries, and partnering with God.

CPSIA information can be obtained
at www.ICGtesting.com
Printed in the USA
LVHW08s0955300818
588639LV00017B/416/P